CW00684231

New Testament Studies

Rudolf Frieling was born in 1901 in Leipzig, Germany. He studied theology and philosophy and took his Ph.D. in Leipzig. He was among those who founded The Christian Community in 1922 and from 1960 until his death in 1986 he was its leader.

Among his works are *Christianity and Reincarnation; Christianity and Islam; Hidden Treasures in the Psalms* and *Old Testament Studies.*

Rudolf Frieling

New Testament Studies

Floris Books

This volume, edited by Tony Jacobs-Brown, was first
published in English by Floris Books in 1994.

Chapters 1–13 were originally published in German under
the title *Bibel-Studien* by Verlag Urachhaus in 1963.
Translated by Margaret and Rudolf Koehler.
Chapters 14–16 were originally published in German as
essays in *Die Christengemeinschaft.* English translations
(Chapters 14 and 15 by Conrad Mainzer, Chapter 16 by Jon
Madsen) were published in the *Threshing Floor.*

'The Transfiguration' was originally published in German
under the title *Die Verklärung auf dem Berge* by Verlag
Urachhaus in 1969. Translated by Hilde Stossel.

'Agape' was originally published in German under the title
Agape. Die göttliche Liebe im Johannes-Evangelium by
Verlag Urachhaus. Third edition 1967. First published in
English by St Norbert Abbey Press, Wisconsin in 1969.
Translated by Jeffrey Kay.

British Library CIP Data available

ISBN 0-86315-185-X

Printed in Great Britain
by Biddles Ltd, Guildford

Contents

Agape — Divine Love in the Fourth Gospel

Preface

The publication of this collection of articles and extended essays on a variety of New Testament themes will stand, along with its companion volume, *Old Testament Studies,** as a worthy memorial and fitting 'testament' to the theological scholarship and spiritual insight of Rudolf Frieling (1901–86), one of the original group of priests responsible for the founding of The Christian Community, a movement for religious renewal taking its inspiration and impulse from the work of Rudolf Steiner (1861–1925).

Frieling was just a young man of twenty-one when the Community was founded and had not yet finished his doctorate, but his talent and stature was soon recognized and he eventually became the leader (erzoberlenker) of The Christian Community, succeeding Friedrich Rittelmeyer and Emil Bock. He was to hold this position for twenty-five years.

Comparison between Frieling and Bock is singularly instructive and reveals the different strengths of these remarkable men. Whereas Bock approaches the Bible in what one might call a 'grand' manner, developing impressive, imaginative panoramas of the vast sweep of cosmic and human evolution, and writes in a style that is fluent and, on occasions, florid, Frieling prefers to focus on the investigation of the biblical text in a more concentratedly exegetical manner. This gives his writing a certain denseness that is at first hard to penetrate, but perseverance will bring its own wonderful rewards.

It is an education in itself to see how Frieling can 'unpack' the inner meaning and significance of a biblical word or phrase

* *Old Testament Studies,* Floris Books, 1987.

and place it in a context that is often surprising but which always feels 'right.' Reading his masterly analyses of certain biblical passages, one realizes the superficiality and lack of spiritual penetration of most orthodox commentaries. This meticulous attention to often the minutest detail of the text is made possible by a philological scholarship second to none and by a special feeling that Frieling possesses for the 'wholeness' of the text he is examining. Thus, not only does he adopt the traditional exegetical approach of seeking for 'parallels' among the so-called Synoptic gospels in order to illuminate a particular passage (what Frieling calls a 'horizontal' reading of the gospels). Such an approach, as Frieling himself points out, can lead to a fragmentation, an 'atomizing,' and a loss of the wholeness of the literary text. Rather, 'to complement the *horizontal* comparison, *vertical* reading must be cultivated, allowing each gospel to stand by itself ... to have its effect as a whole without the distraction of sideways glances to its Synoptic neighbours. Then it becomes clear that ... one and the same event, described in like manner by all three Synoptic gospel writers, assumes a different place value, depending on its position within that particular whole and, depending on possible consonance, a specific tone colour.' Frieling's astonishing analysis of the Transfiguration event, contained in this volume, is a model of such an approach.

In an obituary Michael Tapp summed up the achievement of Rudolf Frieling in a most moving way:

> With Frieling his own modesty and apparent simplicity could almost disguise the depth and the penetration of his insights. He could create vivid images in a single sentence, often breaking into the inner substance of a word and laying it before the hearer in the simplest yet profoundest of ways. One always asked oneself, it's so simple, why couldn't I have thought of that? Of course, it is the kind of simplicity that only comes after all the complications have been worked through. It was not the kind of fundamentalistic simplicity which says 'all you

need to do is believe in Jesus.' It was much more akin
to the simplicity of John's gospel. Rudolf Frieling's
achievement in showing the way forward to a new
Christian spirituality is unique.*

After having read this representative sample of Frieling's
theological legacy, the reader will no doubt find Michael
Tapp's words amply confirmed.

Tony Jacobs-Brown

July 1994

* *The Threshing Floor,* magazine of The Christian Community, February 1986.

Acknowledgments

Quotations from the Bible are from a variety of translations including the Authorised Version, the Revised Standard Version, and the Jerusalem Bible. Where the context requires the author's own translation has been used. These are marked with F after the reference.

Essays on the New Testament

1. Gospel

It is not uncommon to find that people associate the words Evangel* and evangelist with the angels. You could say this is going too far etymologically speaking: 'Evangel,' like 'Gospel,' simply means 'good tidings,' and even *angelos* (from which the second half of the word derives) primarily means 'messenger.' But then — an angel is also a messenger.

For people of ancient times this statement could also be reversed: 'The messenger is an angel.' The basic facts of life were once experienced much more intensely, with all that lay behind them as well. What then is a messenger? Someone who throws a bridge between those who are separated in consciousness from each other. Many people in our own time know what this means: for example, if someone manages to get home with a message for his relations from some far distant prisoner. All human separations are simply consequences of the original separation of human consciousness from the all-embracing divine consciousness into something narrowly circumscribed of its own. With this original separation is connected the fact that we are isolated, 'scattered, every man to his own' (John 16:32, AV). The human being imprisoned in his private individual ego no longer has an immediate knowledge of what goes on in the divine world — nor of what goes on in the souls of his fellow men. People therefore find it exciting and 'inexplicable' when this barrier appears to be raised somewhere and a human being shows a direct knowledge about

* Translator's note: The German language uses the Latin form *Evangelium* for 'Gospel.' The meaning, 'good tidings,' is the same, but it will soon become clear to the reader that the whole tenor of Rudolf Frieling's argument is coloured by this particular form of the word. For this reason the less commonly used English word 'Evangel' has occasionally been used instead of 'Gospel' in this chapter.

something remote from him without any means of external communication. Something like this is only 'inexplicable' as long as we start from the idea that the private, individual consciousness common today was the original state of affairs.

Explaining something means reducing it to such facts as are obvious in themselves and whose evidence satisfies the desire to understand. The history of philosophy shows what difficulties we get into if we take today's 'normal' isolation as if it were a self-evident fact. Then the question arises of how to relate to anything outside ourselves. The truth is, however, that the all-embracing divine consciousness is the original state of things. Ultimately the world comes from *one* divine root, so from the start it is something obvious, self-revelatory, *that everyone knows about everyone.* The isolation, the enclosure in private, circumscribed consciousness only later took shape out of this original unity. It is not the knowledge that reaches into the 'beyond,' not 'telepathy,' that is alarming and inexplicable; it is far more of a riddle how man is able to shut himself up to such an extent within himself. The knowledge of all about all *would* really be something self-evident, needing no clarification, since it is part of the clarity of the all-embracing divine consciousness. What is puzzling and not self-evident is that we do *not* know about each other directly.

This isolated consciousness, far removed from universal sympathy, is the consequence of the Fall. We have separated ourselves from God. We therefore no longer know directly about God and his heavens, about our fellow human beings or the inner life of other creatures. Significantly, the first denial in the Bible of that original knowledge about each other and feeling for each other is expressed by the one who murdered his brother. 'I do not know; am I my brother's keeper?' (Gen.4:9). For the first time someone said, 'I do not know.'

Christ's redemptive deed is to lead the isolated human being out of his prison, and, moreover, with the qualities of personal responsibility and individual freedom made perfect. This breaking down of the limitation of knowing only himself is achieved in the sign of the *Holy Spirit.* Through this extension of consciousness the human being comes into contact with the spiritual world above him, with the *angels.* This in turn allows him to make the first steps in the direction of universal knowledge and universal sympathy, just as on the other hand he can sink into the world below him, into the animal and bestial.

Experience of the Holy Spirit and of angels are therefore intimately connected. So it happens that in the New Testament the Holy Spirit is sometimes represented by the angel. Christ makes this clear (according to Luke 9:26) when he speaks of the threefold glory of his coming again. It will be associated with a new perception of the divine threefoldness: '... when he comes in his (the Son's) glory and the glory of the Father and of the holy angels.' Also in Paul we find: 'In the presence of God and of Christ Jesus and of the elect angels ...' (1Tim. 5:21).

Meeting a messenger on earth is an image of this meeting with angels in a more extended state of consciousness. So from the very beginning the word *angelos* (messenger) also carried with it the sense of 'angel.'

We find the angel-messenger at the very beginning of the Gospel where the angel speaks to Mary and Joseph. First of all, then, there is the *Christmas story.* The actual Christmas events do not lie within the field of 'normal' imprisoned consciousness, which can perceive only that a child is born. What primarily makes Christmas 'Christmas' is on the level of angelic consciousness: '... to you is born this day ... a Savior ...' The Christmas message is in the strictest sense an angelic message — Evangel. It calls for the lifting of the soul above the usual state, opening it towards heaven, to the supersensible. Otherwise there is no true Christmas.

Divine Providence obviously finds it important that this higher, supersensible knowledge is not borne exclusively by angels. That is not enough. Salvation is only complete when those for whom it occurs can become conscious of it. From the beginning Providence sets a high value on the fact that those to be saved are thus 'included' — even if there is only just a minimal awareness on the part of very few human beings. The few in whom the angelic announcement finds a hearing deputize for the whole of humanity. In them humanity turns its eyes heavenward, even when total blindness for the crucial event is otherwise universal.

This is also true of the *Baptism in the Jordan.* The Christ now finally walks on the earthly plane and enters fully into the human vehicle prepared for him, but for humanity imprisoned in its deep soul-sleep this decisive event does not exist — except for one man: John the Baptist. As the 'witness to the light,' he is the opened eye of humanity, its deputizing member, fully conscious, fully awake. Moreover this witnessing is part of the event itself, not only an addition to it.

Where is the angel element here? The appearance of the Baptist is announced by the evangelist with the citation: 'Behold, I send my angel before thee.' Icons picture the Baptist with mighty wings; he acquires the stature of an angel. At the same time, however, he also decidedly belongs to humanity. 'There was a man ... whose name was John.' Man and angel merge in John. Sharing the consciousness of angels enables him to see what simply does not exist for other human beings. According to the Gospel only John, apart from Jesus, saw that heaven opened and the dove descended (John 1:34). The first promise given to Christ's disciples was that they should wake into this angelic awareness of heaven being open (John 1:51). But it appears that this promise referred to a future time, for the disciples' awareness failed again and again. This is particularly noticeable as the event of Golgotha draws near. What happens in the *Garden of Gethsemane* is so tragic because the disciples are inwardly no longer able to follow. They sink into dullness, overpowered by the excessive demand for wakefulness. The necessary minimum of human empathy that Christ expects from at least the three chosen disciples is

16

lacking. The angel therefore has to step in alone and — taking man's place — give Christ the strength that should have come from the disciples' watching and praying with him.

Have people ever really thought how the evangelists could actually describe what Christ experienced after he left the sleepers behind him? There was certainly no further opportunity then when the Lord could have told them — in any case as long as he walked in his mortal body. It can therefore only be a case of supersensible knowledge. What is told of Christ's agony in Gethsemane is again exclusively 'Evangel,' a message of the angels from the supersensible world.

It is only on *Good Friday* that human testimony is again evident. The disciple 'whom the Lord loved' stands beneath the cross and bears witness to what he has seen (John 19:35). At the Baptism it is John the Baptist, and here at Golgotha it is the other John who, as the opened eye of humanity, is part of the event together with the three Marys.

Then the *Resurrection* is such a mighty event — like an intrusion of the Last Day into our own time — that it takes place beyond human awareness. The event itself is without witness, but the result is visible. The disciples do not perceive the Resurrection itself but rather the Risen One — and this only gradually. On Easter morning they are able to see only the 'negative': the empty tomb. As long as human eyes were unseeing, the Easter message was borne alone in the consciousness of the angels until it could be shared by man. 'He has risen' — once more, as at Christmas, an angelic message from the supersensible world. Finally, the disciples themselves share in the visionary consciousness, with differing degrees of certainty (Matt.28:17). At Easter the angel message can finally be confirmed by man. The 'He has risen' of the angel is answered by the testimony of the disciple: 'The Lord has risen indeed' (Luke 24:34). Man can from now on be called 'witness to his resurrection' (Acts 1:22).

In the full sense this comes only after the great spiritual strengthening of *Pentecost*. It is indeed remarkable that during those forty Easter days when the Risen One walked with them the disciples, despite this unique experience, did not yet proclaim it to the rest of the world. Their experience that 'the Lord has risen indeed' had its strength for the time being only within the sheltered inner circle of those who thought and felt the same; it was not yet equal to the cold breath of the rest of the world. But at Whitsun it had reached that stage. By the working of the Holy Spirit the disciples suddenly became preachers who were able to fire the hearts of those standing outside their experience.

In contrast to Christmas and Easter, Whitsun appears to lack the angel element. The appearances of the Risen One introduced by angels come to an end with the two angels of the Ascension — but where are the angels at Whitsun? On this occasion the disciples' consciousness has, by the gifts of the Holy Spirit, so far merged with that of the angels that the angels as it were no longer need to be specially visible and audible. They appear and speak in the spirit-filled disciples who now themselves have become proclaimers of the Gospel — evangelists.

The legend of the Holy Grail describes how the Grail was borne by a group of angels before it found a worthy human keeper in Titurel. This indicates that for a time Christian consciousness on earth had so darkened that once again, as in Gethsemane, the angels deputized for man and had to harbour in their higher spheres the supersensible knowledge of the continued working of the deed of redemption.

Christianity must therefore gain a new insight. The word 'Evangel,' 'Gospel,' will lose its meaning more and more if it does not again acquire the very definite sense of an expansion and raising of human consciousness.

2. The will to be healed

On Chapter Five of John's Gospel

'Do you want to be healed?' This was what Christ asked the sick man at the pool of Bethzatha. One might think it a very strange question for it is surely obvious that the sick man wants to be well. On the other hand one would not like to suppose that the Gospel of John lets Christ ascertain something unimportant and obvious.

Let us look at the setting. There is the pool of Bethzatha with its healing waters welling up from time to time. At the pool are the five porticoes with 'a multitude of invalids' who await the favourable moment — 'blind, lame, paralysed' — all the miseries of humanity are portrayed in this wretched crowd.

If you read the story in Greek you note with surprise that in the course of academic editing the impressive passage about the angel who 'troubles' the water has been crossed out from the text considered authoritative. It is actually missing in some important manuscripts. This could be explained by the fact that in the times when Christianity was beginning to be channelled into ecclesiastical orthodoxy so naive an expression as that about the angel 'troubling' the water could have been felt as a possible encouragement of 'heathen' nature worship. But does not the Apocalypse, the Revelation of the same John, know of an angel who is specially in command of the waters? (Rev.16:5).

It is the very movement of the water bubbling up from time to time (the original text here uses the word *kairos*) that gives the opportunity for an invisible spiritual being to take shape, as it were, in it, or rather 'on' it. One would not actually want to use the word 'embody.' It is a case of an angel very fleetingly taking bodily form by means of a suitable physical phenomenon. Water was always regarded by the ancients as such a phenomenon — especially when it was not stagnant, 'dead' water but was alive with movement, springing up, rippling and splashing.

They experienced angels as moving up and down. The forefather Jacob saw this in his nocturnal vision of the heavenly ladder. Christ also speaks of this to his disciples at the beginning of his ministry (John 1:51). When they 'ascend,' they carry up to higher worlds what is ripe for heaven. When they 'descend,' they permeate what is receptive on earth with the blessing that comes from above. So when the moment of grace, the *kairos*, is given, the angel of the pool of Bethzatha carries down healing forces from a higher realm and momentarily makes the bubbling water the medium of etheric activity.

Water plays a special part in the imagery of the myths and tales that arose from ancient clairvoyance, which is even reflected in the popular saying about the stork picking up babies from the pool. Men on earth, estranged from their heavenly origin, fallen into sickness and frailty — are they not in this sense really 'left high and dry'? But the pool of Bethzatha (Hebrew: 'house of grace') with the mystery of its angel still somehow links them with their original condition at the time of creation.

Nevertheless, with a significant diminution. Only the one who steps in first finds restoration to the original state of God-given health. 'Whoever stepped in first.' This is no more a popular superstition to be excused by the modern reader than the descending angel. It rather quite realistically indicates a field of experience fraught with problems. We can find a key to it if, for example, we consider the following. Suppose the overwrought city-dweller in need of recuperation makes an excursion into the neighbouring countryside — let us say on Monday. Everywhere he encounters the unpleasant traces of the thousands who swarmed there the previous weekend. It is not only that the 'disfigurement' of nature by the scattered remains offends the eye; even if all the trippers have gone away leaving everything tidy, there still remains the impression that something destructive must have passed over the landscape. Meadows and trees look almost like lifeless pasteboard scenery, the lovely green world seems to have had its vital forces simply 'sucked out.' In the course of the week, if it is left to itself, it slowly regains something of them, until the next 'sucking out.' Whoever can, therefore, seeks for recuperation in a part of the countryside as much as possible undisturbed by man, in which something of the divine quality of nature can still be felt. Not everyone is in this position, however. Let him for whom it *is* possible be thankful, but not without giving the matter some thought. He can gain strength from the undisturbed divine forces of nature for the very reason that 'the others' are not there. The moment those others, his fellow men, were to come, if only in hundreds — to say nothing of the hundreds of thousands and millions — the healing power would be done for. It can, then, always be comparatively few who are restored to health at this fountain of youth. It goes relentlessly according to the rule: 'Who comes first is healed — the others are the losers.' The sick man of the pool of Bethzatha had belonged for many long years to those at a disadvantage in the race. He waited habitually, though having almost given up hope that it would one day be his privilege to come first.

And now comes Christ and takes a quite different approach. What is decisively new about his miracle? The sick man, stuck fast in his thoughts, can only say: '... I have no man to put me into the pool when the water is troubled, and while I am going another steps down before me.' This is the only way he knows how to answer the question, 'Do you want to be healed?' But Christ does not go into that; he does not provide for someone to carry the sick man to the water in time. Instead he calls upon his innermost being. This call to the will sleeping in the depths of his being nevertheless first of all receives only the man's hopelessly resigned answer. The mood of weariness that has become chronic in the course of years of disappointment still runs on almost automatically. But one could imagine that while this went on on the surface of consciousness, Christ's words, 'Do you want to be healed?' had already stirred a positive reaction in the depths of the soul. The sick man would not otherwise have been able to respond to Christ's next words, 'Rise, take up your pallet and walk,' by actually shaking off his disability. Without recourse to the pool of Bethzatha he found health and uprightness through what had taken place between his innermost being and Christ.

This opens up a wide perspective for the future. It will become more and more evident that the healing needed by human beings can no longer be adequately supplied by physical means. It will be more and more important what sort of relationship they establish towards Christ. This is where the *will* for being healthy comes in.

There are two possibilities of dealing wrongly with this will. On the one hand there is the danger that it is weakened from within. Being ill can very easily become disastrously associated with egoism. Thus some people become interesting to themselves with their illness, become totally absorbed in this self-centred interest and expect everyone they meet to share it. Being ill, with the associated privileged treatment, accustoms many patients to enjoy a kind of special position. In this way the sincere will for normal health, entailing once more the prosaic daily tasks that no one notices, is greatly weakened. It also happens that people actually 'flee' from difficult situations into being ill. This begins comparatively harmlessly with the schoolchild who longs for a bit of influenza when faced with the fatal work test. It can later grow into a real 'deserter' attitude in the face of the difficulties of life.

Therefore, the question, 'Do you want to be healed?' in no way implies something that is a matter of course.

The will for good health that Christ inspires in men is also always the will for fulfilling life's duties. It is not for nothing that Christ commands the man who has been healed to carry away the pallet on which he lay. There is something deeply

symbolical in this. The man is no longer someone who is a
burden but who should now get used to taking up and carrying
burdens himself — he who was himself in need of being
carried.

On the other hand though the will to be healthy can be quite
sincere, egoism can still creep in to adulterate it; it becomes a
self-centred striving simply for physical strength and is only
out for what one could call an animal state of health. In
Christ's sense bodily restoration is to be only incidental to an
inner healing, an inner rising from the fall into sin. The story
of the sick man at the pool of Bethzatha has a sequel. Christ
'finds' the man afterwards in the Temple. He knows how to
find him, he knows how to meet him again at the right
moment in order to confirm and complete what has gone
before. It is a meeting in the privacy of the holy place. The
man is made aware: 'See, you are well!' From this awareness
is to be born a new will. The will that was first called upon for
the restoration of the body is raised into the sphere of higher
aims, and now appears in its true and profoundest form. The
'Do you want to be healed?' changes in Christ's third utterance into 'Sin no more ...' Overcome the sickness of sin with
your will!

The actual time of the event at Bethzatha can also tell us
something. It was then 'the' feast of the Jews (as good
readings say), and according to the usage of the time that
meant the autumn Feast of Tabernacles following the great Day
of Atonement. It happened therefore in the autumn — we
would say in a Michaelic atmosphere. In autumn we are more
particularly concerned with our inner life, and so it is at
Michaelmas time that we experience the question, 'Do you
want to be healed?' in all its seriousness; we take pains to
answer it sincerely with 'Yes' so that Christ can approach us
with his healing will and restore in us the image of man willed
by God.

3. The healing under the opened roof
Mark 2:1–12

Among the accounts of healings there is one that is particularly impressive in the picture it puts before us. It is that of the paralytic whom his bearers let down to the Saviour through the opened roof because the crowd prevented them from reaching him in any other way.

'... Jesus saw their faith ...' He saw that it was the deep commitment of their hearts to the divine that made them inventive and prompted this original idea. By this strange action they presented a symbolic picture of a significant fact.

In small children the top of the skull still has a weak spot; the 'fontanel' in the top of the head is not yet closed. Parallel with this is the fact that the child is not yet cut off from the world of his heavenly origin. The soul is not yet fully drawn into the house of the body; it still keeps open its connection with heaven, even if only when sleeping and dreaming. The hardening of the skull is the visible expression of what then gradually comes about: the door towards heaven is closed and the soul wakes into sense-awareness of the earthly world.

In the cripple whom the four men bring to Christ there lives a soul that has forgotten its eternal origin, being too much under the spell of earthly existence. It has become entangled in grievous sin and has fallen too far from the world in which it once had the angels for its companions. Nevertheless the sick man has an instinctive feeling that in Christ Jesus someone has appeared through whom all can be made well again. Through him can again be established what apparently lies so unattainably remote: the still uninjured, divine freshness and purity of the child on its way from heaven and only just parting company with the angels. This belief is shared by those who carry him. And so they embark on their extraordinary deed; they take the roof off so that the meeting comes about with the blue sky looking into the closed chamber and the breath of the divine worlds blowing in unhindered.

Christ 'knew what was in man.' He sees directly into this man and his destiny, his estrangement from heaven and his painful homesickness for the good and holy. Before he deals with the bodily ailment, he heals the soul. His comforting pronouncement begins with an unusual salutation. How does he address this man? 'My child!' (Literal translation of the Greek text).

We should be aware that a similar address is reported nowhere else in the Gospels. Where Christ addresses an individual grown man he calls him by his name, or even calls him 'man,' or, in the case of a woman, 'woman' or 'my daughter.'

In rare cases Christ addresses the disciples all together as 'children,' even 'little children.' This is far from being sentimental or 'preachy,' but has very real meaning. It is chosen because in the higher sense it is factually correct when he addresses what is only just beginning to grow in the disciples, what is hidden behind their apparent maturity — the undeveloped future man. As the apostles see the rich young man turn away, the man who could not bring himself to leave the past behind him, who, burdened by wealth, sinned against his future — then Christ addresses them as 'children' (Mark 10:24). After the washing of the feet Christ calls the disciples 'little children' as he proceeds to set before them the 'new commandment' of love (John 13:33). The Risen One asks the disciples in the boat: 'Little children, have you nothing to eat?' (John 21:5F). By means of the wonderful draft of fish he gives them the holy breakfast which nourishes the future man in them, the 'little child.'

But that he says 'my child' to an individual happens only with the paralytic when the sky is visible through the opened roof. It is precisely to *him* that he says it, the one who has so alienated himself from his child nature and become a sinner. The Christ may indeed say it, for he is able to take upon himself the 'sins' that darken the child in this man, and deal with them as a god.

The scribes are not essentially in the wrong when they object: 'Who can forgive sins but God alone?' They know that when man sins he always 'puts himself in debt.' Indeed he does something beyond all human possibility of reparation to a higher world, ultimately to God himself. And that can only be put right by a deed on the part of the one to whom it has been done, by a revelation of the very Godhead of what he is, which creates a new state of affairs through the power of sacrifice. Only God can take away sin — but, as the scribes know, 'God is in heaven.' Yet here stands Jesus of Nazareth as an earthly man and says: 'My child, your sins are forgiven.' How can he usurp God's prerogative? The scribes do not see that something greater than a man stands before them. In him heaven has come to earth. The power of healing sin has been brought down into the human realm by God's having become man.

Therefore Christ can say that 'the Son of *Man* has authority on *earth* to forgive sins.' This is what is new. And he proves this power in public by adding to the healing of the soul quite logically the healing of the body. He tells the paralysed man to stand up and walk.

4. The rich man and death
Luke 12:16–21

The story of the rich man and poor Lazarus is well known. Less well known on the whole is another parable that also deals with the death of a rich man and also occurs in Luke's Gospel. It is very concise, a really 'short story,' but the few sentences are momentous and are worth a really detailed study.

'The land of a rich man brought forth plentifully ...' So it begins. Before this particularly fortunate harvest the owner was therefore well-off. Now he becomes richer than before. And just as the poor have their troubles, so do the well-to-do. The enormous yield comes as an embarrassment to him. Where shall he put it all?

'... and he thought to himself, "What shall I do, for I have nowhere to store my crops"?' Then the idea comes to him: 'And he said, "I will do this: I will pull down my barns, and build larger ones; and there I will store all my grain and my goods".'

What does it say in the soliloquy? 'My crops — my barns — my grain — my goods.' My — my — my — my. 'My barns' — that may pass. But 'my crops' — 'my grain'? He apparently does not consider that with all his wealth he cannot produce a single blade of grass. What grows and ripens is a gift of grace from the divine creative powers.

The soliloquy, however, is not yet finished. After the rich landowner has thought of his plan of action, he anticipates with self-satisfaction the agreeable state of his own soul in the future. 'And I will say to my soul, Soul, you have ample goods laid up for many years; take your ease, eat, drink, be merry.' — Again the possessive 'my': 'my soul.' It is true that in the same Gospel Mary says this in her song of praise, the

Magnificat: 'My soul magnifies the Lord ...' But when two people say the same thing, it is not the same.

'Rest, eat and drink, be cheerful.' The Gospel would not object to these things in themselves. Indeed they are honoured throughout the Gospels.

'Rest.' Anyone who is able to draw breath again in peace after the pressure of hard work can have a direct experience of something 'heavenly.' For the hardworking man such tranquil drawing of breath can become a religious experience that allows him to sense something of the peacefully breathing life of the divine. The same verb, *(anapauein),* occurs in the passionate cry of the Saviour that goes forth to 'all who labour and are heavy-laden': I will refresh you, I will give you this heavenly rest. With the rich man in the parable, however, this resting, taking his ease, acquires quite a different character. In *his* programme it signifies quite simply the final dismissal of every desire to work, the letting go of every readiness to exert himself, the intention to live only for himself. The experience of rest is thus denuded of its heavenly connotations and degenerates into simply 'doing nothing.'

'Eat and drink.' It is the same here. In a healthy, natural working life eating and drinking, preceded by hunger and thirst, can also be a religious experience. It can become symbolic for satisfaction on a higher level. 'O taste and see that the Lord is good!' says one of the Psalms. When grace is said, eating and drinking are consciously raised to the level of religious devotion. In the sacrament it undergoes its highest transformation. At the opposite pole stands the 'eat and drink' of the rich man who has settled down to take his ease. For him eating and drinking is an end in itself, an important part of his programme for enjoying life. Thus it falls away from its higher potential and is lost in the purely material.

'Be merry.' Again one could not advance arguments from the Gospels against being gay and cheerful. This is shown particularly well by the three Luke parables about losing and finding (Luke 15). The shepherd who has found his sheep again, the woman who has found her silver coin — both call their friends and neighbours together. 'Rejoice with me ...' These are small events in the lives of simple people. But Christ had a loving eye for how often it was just the simple person involved in the struggle for existence who preserved a special capacity for cheerfulness. The finding of the sheep and the silver coin, in themselves no world-shaking events, become the occasion for great rejoicing, whereby despite their poor and modest circumstances people are glad of heart. Higher things can be revealed through them. 'Even so, I tell you, there will be ... joy in heaven ... Even so ... there is joy before the angels of God ...' Christ Jesus felt for the poor, but he could regard with equal warmth a man who was rich in worldly goods. It is not the fact of possession itself that is reprehensible. However, it is pointed out again and again in the Gospels, often very radically, that there is a danger of the soul being enslaved by ownership if it does not watch out. It is the state of mind dominated by possessions that is warned against. This is epitomized in the rich man in our parable. In contrast, a sympathetically drawn rich man is found in the parable of the Prodigal Son. There the father is described as a landowner who has a great fortune at his disposal, who has numerous hired servants in his service who all 'have bread enough and to spare.' In this man Christ lets us see the fatherly kindness of God in an earthly model. Here, too, is the great feast of rejoicing, with singing and dancing. 'It is fitting to make merry and be glad, for this your brother was dead, and is alive; he was lost, and is found.'

Again, in the case of the rich man in our parable, being merry, just like resting and eating and drinking, has degenerated into an end in itself. The same idea of making merry, that sounds so differently on the lips of the lazy landowner and the father of the prodigal son, also occurs in the story of poor Lazarus, where the rich man 'was clothed in purple and fine linen and ... feasted sumptuously every day.' But in this kind of pleasure taking there is not a single gleam of heavenly joy, and after his death the man who every day lived so pleasurably finds himself in the purifying flames of burning desire, since in his enjoyment anything resembling the life of the spirit was blotted out.

'Rest, eat, drink, enjoy yourself!' So much for the rich man's soliloquy. And now begins the parable's other part. 'But God said to him ...' In no other parable are the words of God himself introduced so directly, so undisguised. In other parables the lord of the vineyard perhaps speaks the decisive word, or the master of the house, the bridegroom, the king, and we sense the higher being they represent. Here, however, it says with astonishing directness: 'But God said to him ...'

But how is one to think of this speaking of God to the rich man? He was quite evidently no mystic, no pious religious who listens with devotion to divine revelations and is blessed with inspiration. God speaks to him through destiny. He makes him die a sudden death.

A man can fall into a singular mood before his 'unexpected' death, a death which is in no way to be foreseen. Perhaps he is suddenly overcome by an unusual sadness, an inexplicable feeling of farewell, or by a strange agitation; perhaps he makes a strange remark. All quite unmotivated, as one thinks. In fact, however, such occurrences furnish intrinsic evidence of the fact that the 'unexpected' death was not so unexpected after all. Something in the man already knew. It is only that this knowledge already there in the bottom of the soul could not yet rise up into the light of full consciousness. So it made itself felt in a different way in the soul.

Thus in the day before the tragic event the rich man also heard in the deeper levels of his soul God's pronouncement of his fate.

And the content of this divine utterance? First: 'Fool!' The Greek word denotes someone who is without reason, without sense. This word resounding towards him from the divine world contains the judgment of the life he has lived till now, and which now faces its end. This existence, envied and considered happy by many people, is scathingly judged by a higher court.

Secondly there follows the announcement of the catastrophe. 'This night your soul is required of you.' Nothing is described in detail in this austere parable. We do not discover in what form the catastrophe will occur. All the more sinister are the words 'this night.' There is divine mastery in the telling of this story which in a few words conjures up a whole world of experience. This night ... the Gospel also speaks of the blessing of night, which is dark only to keep away the glaring brightness of day and make the soul receptive for a different kind of light. But here only the darkness of night is left. It is the lightless night that is no one's friend. 'This night your soul is required of you.' Who will take his life remains unknown, which makes it all the more terrible and full of foreboding. One could think of a murderer. 'Your soul is required ...' is ambiguous. It may imply murder, but at the same time it also leaves open another meaning. The murder can in the end only kill the body. The disembodied soul goes into the hands of higher powers who demand back through the fatal event the soul they once sent down to earth.

'Your soul ...' However short the parable, there is yet room for literary counterpoint. We are reminded of the self-satisfied words: 'I will say to my soul ...' Now there comes like an echo from the divine world: 'This soul of yours' ... which you looked upon as a private possession, which will now be demanded back by its true owner.

The divine message contains a third element: 'and the things you have prepared, whose will they be?' What was hoarded in order to guarantee a life of enjoyment 'for many years' must be left behind. If his earthly possessions were all in all to a man, then it must be terrible for him to meet the question: 'To whom will they belong now?'

The coming of death is announced in a threefold way: the existence that has come to an end is assessed and judged by a higher court; the soul is demanded back by the divine powers;

the earthly goods pass on elsewhere. There the curtain falls. We are not, however, dismissed simply with the shock of the sudden disaster. Being shocked makes us receptive for the saying that takes up the strain of the story that has just ended: 'So is he who lays up treasure for himself, and is not rich toward God.' There arises the ideal of striving for *that* treasure. 'Be rich in God.' Then death loses its terror.

5. The Holy Spirit in the light of the predictions of Christ's Passion

The deed of redemption on Golgotha includes not only the Passion and Death but also the Resurrection. The Death and Resurrection of Christ are indivisibly bounds together and form the 'Mystery of Golgotha.' That is not all, however. More careful consideration reveals that yet a third element is involved. The full effect of the Death and Resurrection of Christ depends upon whether they are really taken to heart by humanity. To the Death and Resurrection there must be added the third element of their becoming manifest to humanity.

This can be brought about by the Holy Spirit, which can so illumine consciousness that the event of Golgotha permeates the thinking, feeling and willing of Christians.

If we want to gain some idea of this illumination by the Holy Spirit, it can be helpful to look also at what is contained in the Gospels as a sort of 'negative picture' of it.

Matthew, Mark and Luke hand down to us what are called the predictions of the Passion. There are certainly also isolated hints, but the three predictions of the Passion have something like a religious solemnity in their foretelling of the event of Golgotha. They indicate how important it was for Christ that at least a small circle of people should be prepared for it with understanding and sympathy when it happened. The predictions of the Passion, which also already include the Resurrection, are meant to serve that 'becoming manifest' mentioned above. Only — tragically — they do not find the right response. The Holy Spirit is able to work directly for mankind only after Golgotha, from Whitsun on. Thus each time lack of understanding follows the predictions, the 'negative' of what would have been enlightenment.

The *first* prediction of the Passion takes place in about the last summer of Christ's ministry. In time and even place this is a long way from Golgotha. Christ is making a lonely journey with the disciples which has led them out of Palestine into the north, into the foothills of the snow covered range of Mount Hermon in the region of Caesarea Philippi. After being absorbed in prayer on his own (Luke 9:18), Christ questions the disciples about who he is. What do people say? What do *they* say? Peter is then inspired to say something, the import of which he himself is unable to see. 'You are the Christ, the Son of the living God' (Matt.16:16). As if he would say: 'Now you shall also understand what you have said,' Christ proceeds to the first prediction of his Passion. Withdrawn from the world, in time and place still far from Golgotha, he reveals to the disciples the principle of the divine necessity of suffering. It is a 'must' of a higher kind: he 'must' go to Jerusalem and there 'suffer many things.' The authorities will reject and condemn him. He will be killed and rise again on the third day.

As an answer to this on the part of the disciples there comes only Peter's reaction. It is one of 'aversion.' Though he has just been privileged to speak the glorious confession, he has now sunk back again into his still unchanged, 'all too human' nature. He therefore protests: 'God forbid, Lord! This shall never happen to you' (Matt.16:22).

A week later Peter, together with two other disciples, is privileged to be a witness of the Transfiguration. Soon after that — now in Galilee (Matt.17:22) — there follows the *second* prediction. It has a different character from the first. Once the remote loneliness of the Mount Hermon range has been left behind, we have already in Galilee come nearer to the arena of the forthcoming event. This now comes closer. The second prediction is the shortest. It does not go into the kind of suffering, but includes the whole Passion in the expression that the Son of Man 'is to be delivered into the hands of men.' In Luke's version this is, in fact, the only statement in this prediction (Luke 9:44). In the Transfiguration Christ Jesus had shone as the living monstrance, as the Host irradiated by the sun. Now the second prediction of his Passion introduces the picture of men's hands reaching out for this Host — though here are meant the hands of murderers. But if the sinful hands had not murderously seized the Saviour, there would not have been the possibility for men to receive into their hands the Host, the bread as the body of Christ, through the Eucharist — therein lies the paradox of the deed of Golgotha. It is this very picture of the Saviour 'delivered into the hands of men' that Christ wants to impress upon the feelings of his disciples.

Luke has a special sense for nuances of feeling, for mysteries of the soul. It is he who paints the picture of Mary, who preserves Christ's saying about hearing as a fructifying of the soul (8:11-15; 11:28), who hands down the saying: 'Take heed ... how you hear' (8:18). Thus there is a special ring to it when the Gospel of Luke introduces the second prediction of the Passion with the words: 'Let these words sink into your ears ...' Yet the expected sympathetic understanding is lacking. 'But they did not understand this saying, and it was concealed from them, that they should not perceive it, and they were afraid to ask him about this saying' (9:45). The disciples could not 'perceive' this saying. Matthew supplements this. 'And they were greatly distressed' is the way he describes the disciples' reaction to this second prediction (17:23). Instead of the appropriate sympathetic understanding that can boldly face the tragedy of the Passion and Death since it is able to rise to the super-earthly joy of the Resurrection — instead of this emotional strength to cope with the very depths and heights of feeling, there proceeds from their inadequate response only a dull and paralysing general misery.

The *third* prediction of the Passion occurs already very close in place and time to what has been foretold. Christ is going up to Jerusalem to his last Passover and is already in Judea, before Jericho.

It is always the case with pre-vision that the pictures become more detailed and precise the nearer the coming event approaches. The third prediction therefore already contains details of being delivered up to the heathen, that is to the Romans, the specific features of being mocked and spat upon, the scourging, and, for the first time — if we follow Matthew — also the manner of death in the form of crucifixion (20:19). 'Everything ... will be accomplished ...' (Luke 18:31). It is all characterized by an element of will. 'Behold, we are going up to Jerusalem.' Mark describes Christ's heroic walking ahead whilst his disciples follow with trepidation (Mark 10:32). This time, however, the disciples' powers of perception are even more clouded than before. This is expressed in a threefold way by Luke: 'But they understood none of these things; this saying was hid from them, and they did not grasp what was said' (18:34). The lack of understanding never sounded so complete. The disciples 'understood' nothing — in Greek this suggests: 'They did not bring it together.' They could not intellectually grasp it, they were unable to put death and resurrection together in one picture. They could not combine all this with the ideas of Christ they had formed up to that time. It remains 'hidden' from them. Finally, that unique and impressive word for 'grasp': *ginōskein.* But negative: 'they did not grasp ...'

From this negative counter-image it can become clear what we hope for from the Holy Spirit. It will make this understanding possible. Then nothing remains 'hidden,' but the hidden mystery is able to become an open mystery; for it remains a mystery even when it is understood, indeed all the more so. Just as the better I know a person the more, not less, of a mystery he becomes to me. Then, too, enlightened by the Spirit, we are able to unite in our souls the apparently incompatible agony of death and glory of resurrection. Then paralysing sadness is replaced by Easter joy, the rejoicing in spirit, if the soul can immerse itself in the event of Golgotha and experience it as it is worthy of being experienced. Then finally the resistance to suffering is replaced by the joyful readiness to carry the cross as a follower of Christ, in order to participate in the agony of his Passion and Death and in his Resurrection.

Through the Holy Spirit the disciples' threefold failure over the predictions of the Passion can gradually be made good and changed into its opposite. The event of Golgotha can only be fully effective if it is seen as comprising the trinity of Christ's Passion, his Resurrection and his becoming manifest.

6. Three parables about Christ's future coming

In Christ's discourse on the Mount of Olives we hear the great Advent Gospel of the future coming of the Son of Man in the etheric light and the clouds of heaven. Matthew's Gospel has preserved for us three parables that form the conclusion of this apocalyptic discourse and at the same time answer the question how we should behave in relation to this coming. They are the pictures of the ten maidens, the talents and the last judgment.

First picture: the wise and foolish maidens

The character of this parable already reveals itself in its title, and depends on the two words 'wise' and 'foolish.' The wise maidens have thought about fuel for their lamps with which they are to meet the bridegroom. The foolish let their lamps go out since they have not bothered about oil.

It is the contrast of 'spiritually alert' and 'spiritually dull,' the one responsible, the other irresponsible towards the light.

The picture of the 'bridegroom' who comes only at 'midnight' still reflected for people of those days something of the mysteries. The bridegroom is he to whom the soul should be completely devoted. He is the man that shines at midnight. Essentially he is light, but pure inner light which shines brightest when the glare of outer light has faded and the soul's deeper faculties emerge — 'at midnight.'

The maidens go to meet this bringer of divine light, and it is important that they go to meet him with lighted lamps. Light wants to be welcomed with light. The outer physical light can illumine what is dark and so make it bright. The inner light, however, does not simply light superficially. It seeks to *en*lighten; but to do so it must be able to be inwardly welcomed. This is only possible when its like is already there. In Goethe's tale of the Green Snake the 'old man with the lamp' pronounces the law that only like recognizes like with the words: 'You know that I may not light up what is dark.'

When the one who is entitled to call himself 'the light of the world' is coming, it is therefore not enough to wait passively for him. We should go to meet him, we should bestir ourselves, we should carry the light to meet him, the light already given us, which is there for our use — if we take care of it and do not let it fail.

The human soul's power of pure thinking has something virginal about it. The ancient Greeks revered the virgin goddess, Pallas Athene, who sprang forth from the head of Zeus. This power of inner brightness and clarity of perception has also been recognized in early Christian tradition as the holy 'Sophia.' The virgin in the Gospel who meets the bringer of light with lighted lamp can be seen as an image of this 'Sophia.'

Second picture: the talents

Quite a different kind of imagery dominates the second parable. There are no maidens here, but men, servants of their master, used to hard work. Their lord has entrusted them with his property, giving to each a number of talents. The very word 'talent' suggests the possibility for action: man may put his talents to work.

The master's property is handed over in individually proportioned amounts; one gets more, the other less, but the chief thing is that no one goes without; everyone gets something. Every man is given something of what is God's own. One is able to do more, another less, but no one is quite incapable; everyone can do something. It all depends on the one who 'can' do only a little in all modesty working with even this little. This is much more important than looking askance at another who can do more and, at the sight of his advantage, getting an inferiority complex which basically — paradoxical as it sounds — often simply springs from unconscious vanity; for it is really a lack of modesty if one does not quite objectively accept the little one has, in order to work all the more diligently with it. So the two sayings, 'Do what you can' and 'What you can do, get on and do!' are both valid in this respect.

Just as a person is responsible that the light given him does not go out, so he should increase the talent given to him by his hard work. He is not only to meet the divine with the perceptive power of his thinking, he is also to offer it his ability to work, his energy.

The religious life must again acquire something of the seriousness and the method of real 'work.' It cannot be an unprofessional pursuit of an occasional Sunday religious mood; it needs the sustained will, the energy of hard work. How splendid and accurate is the old-fashioned expression, 'religious practice'!

The two servants who have increased what was entrusted to them 'enter into the joy of their Lord.' The third, however, puts what was entrusted to him in the earth — the picture of a man who invests all his energy in the transitoriness of earthly things or, better expressed, 'buries it.' Thereby he robs himself of the great experience of joy shared by those who have really 'worked' spiritually.

Third picture: the Last Judgment

The first two parables address themselves to human thinking and to human will. They say: You owe your thinking and your working ability to the divine. Take care of the light that is given you and work according to your abilities, and then you prepare yourself worthily for the midnight coming of the bridegroom, for returning an account to the Lord when he requires it. The third picture, the account of the Last Judgment, adds something more of the greatest importance.

It begins straight away with the motif of the coming of the Son of Man in revealing light: 'When the Son of Man comes in his glory, and all the angels with him, then he will sit on his glorious throne.' Once enthroned, he is called 'the King' (Matt. 25:34). He judges men according to whether they have shown mercy or not. '... as you did it to one of the least of these my brethren, you did it to me.'

It is not here a case of particular types of humanity, ('maiden,' 'manservant'), of man and woman, but of the purely human itself. This time the emphasis lies not upon the alertness of the spirit (although the deeds of mercy will be done 'with understanding'), nor on the energetic will to work (although the deeds of mercy have to be wrested from inertia). The opposites this time are not 'wise and foolish,' not 'hard-working and lazy,' but 'merciful and unmerciful.' It is here a matter of the truly human feeling of the heart that experiences others as the brothers of Christ.

The series of three pictures therefore speaks of thinking, willing and feeling. It indicates that the future coming of Christ can only be our salvation if it can find some inner connection with us, if it meets what we have prepared for it in the way of pure, spiritually orientated thinking, active will, and heartfelt love.

The differences between the three parables stand out more sharply if for a moment we look at the 'negative' pictures. Each parable contains its 'negative'; we are told of the unfortunate fate of the foolish maidens, the lazy servant, and the unmerciful.

Each time a different punishment comes into force. Closer observation, however, shows that they are not exactly 'punishments' imposed from without. It is unmistakable how in each case those concerned bring about their own fate, how each time, therefore, the punishment with intrinsic logic suits the offence.

What happens to the *foolish virgins?* They stand in front of the closed door which will not be opened again for them. The bridegroom answers their knocking with: 'I do not know you.'

The closed door indicates something significant. A door is a wall that can cease to be a wall, a wall that can allow the view to open into a space not previously perceptible. Whoever lets his light of perception fail finally runs against the wall of the boundaries of knowledge built up by the merely earthly, intellectual consciousness; he then notices: Only behind this wall lies the real thing, but no door will open. The impotence of perception in the face of what is finally recognized as the meaning and value of existence, the supersensible, is painfully experienced as his own guilt, since he has negligently allowed his light to go out.

In the spirit, all knowledge is at the same time a 'being known.' Anyone who never strives to know the divine does not shine in the world above as a spiritual form. He does not perceive, and is therefore not perceived. 'I perceive you not' or 'I know you not' (as it says in Matt.25:12).

The *lazy servant* is cast out into the 'darkness' where 'men will weep and gnash their teeth.' He who buries his will in transitory, worldly things is left to the misfortune of a merely physical existence, which from a spiritual point of view is darkness. The soul 'weeps' in uncontrolled pain since in its desolate egoism it is a burden and a pain to itself, whilst the ego, 'gnashing its teeth,' grows harder and more cramped in the 'death of matter.'

The *unmerciful,* however, are consigned to the fire. The fire of hell is not here described in the gruesome way unfortunately so common in a crude and very dubious form of 'Christianity.' Here in the Gospel's austere parable about hell-fire, we are able to look at the original picture, free of erroneous associations. Again, it is not 'punishment' imposed from without by

a vengeful judge, but basically a self-induced consequence. At
the end of Goethe's *Faust* we see the Devil and his crew take
to flight before the divine fire of love. The very element that
is bliss to the good inflicts pain on the evil. It is one and the
same fire. As far as God is concerned, it is only love. The
Godhead cannot be other than itself; it subsists in the fire of
love. He who places himself outside this love feels it as a
tormenting reproach when he meets it. He suffers in the fire
that burns to the torment of the Devil and his angels. Those
who have stifled the voice of their hearts bring this torment
upon themselves. For the merciful, however, the return of the
'king,' before whose throne man is finally judged by his
worthiness or unworthiness, opens the way to 'eternal life.'

7. The seven Easter stories in the Gospels

It strikes us again and again how Providence, rather than Chance, has brought the four Gospels together. We do not, for example, find the 'seven words from the cross' complete in any one Gospel, but together the four give us this precious legacy. It is the same with the description of events after the Resurrection.

How many appearances of the Risen One are actually recorded — not just mentioned, but fully described? First there is the experience of the women, particularly Mary Magdalene, in the early morning at the grave. In the afternoon, the journey to Emmaus. In the evening, the appearance to the disciples behind locked doors. One week later, the appearance for Thomas in particular. There are two further appearances in Galilee, not precisely dated, one on the mountain, one by the lake. Finally, the last appearance to the disciples linked with the Ascension. Exactly seven. It is apparent that these were not the only ones. Paul mentions appearances to Peter (also mentioned by Luke), to James, to 'five thousand brethren.' But only the seven are actually described and given in detail.

Can this be accidental? If we try to perceive the special character, the particular mood of each of these seven stories, we can come to the feeling that the same 'seven' is involved as in the 'seven planets' spoken of by ancient wisdom. This tradition has been corroborated by Rudolf Steiner's spiritual research and seen in a new way; it is correct, notwithstanding our modern astronomy. It concerns the working of cosmic forces in seven different ways, known of old to be connected with Moon, Venus, Mercury, Sun, Mars, Jupiter and Saturn — those of Venus and Mercury being interchangeable.

The women at the grave

The women are the first in whom there awoke a clairvoyant perception of the Risen One. The *Moon,* understood not merely as a 'heavenly body' but as a special field of forces, has a special connection with the feminine. As the moon sickle can appear as a bowl of silver, so may the 'feminine' in men become a vessel to receive the 'sun'-light of Christ. The weeping Mary Magdalene, whose deep sorrow becomes the eye whereby she sees the risen Master who completely fulfills her devoted soul — this is a revelation of the noblest possibilities of the lunar quality of the soul.

On the way to Emmaus

There is a different mood in the story of the two disciples who walk to Emmaus. They are also very sad, though their sadness is not so much the personal, heartfelt pain of Mary Magdalene — it is rather caused by mental suffering. As they talk, they struggle to comprehend the incomprehensible, of which they were witnesses on Good Friday. Their sincere search for the truth makes it possible for the 'third' to join them. Whilst walking with them 'on the way,' he illumines their understanding. He teaches them to grasp the secret meaning of holy scripture. 'Was it not necessary that the Christ should suffer these things ...?' This 'was it not necessary?' makes a divine demand upon the human power of understanding. The Death and Resurrection of Christ are not an incomprehensible miracle that one blindly accepts. 'Was it not necessary? ...' opens the way to seeing what in a higher sense is 'to be seen.'

Here we feel something of the quality of *Mercury,* of Hermes. The Greeks regarded him as the messenger of the gods with winged shoes, 'on the way' between gods and men in order to serve understanding between them. The art of interpretation or exposition, which makes clear 'what is meant,' is called 'hermeneutics.' The corresponding verb, *hermēneuō,* actually occurs in the original Greek text. He 'interpreted to them in all the scriptures, ...' reads: *di-hermēneusen* (Luke 24:27). The Christ walking with the two is like a more sublime Mercury.

Easter evening

The Easter evening story, especially as it is described by John (20:19-23), seems as if drenched in the element of spiritual love. (The parallel accounts in Mark 16 and Luke 24 clearly give rather a summary of the whole forty days leading up to the Ascension.) On this occasion 'Peace be with you' is said for the first time after the Resurrection. The disciples respond with joy. The Risen One shows them the marks of the wounds of his great deed of love. He breathes on them and so lets them share for the first time in the Holy Spirit so that they can heal the sickness of sin. *Venus,* once the star of 'Lucifer,' is Christianized. Venus Urania, the heavenly love, is here at work between Christ and his disciples. (In the sense of the above-mentioned interchange, one can also feel in this 'healing of the sickness of sin' a Mercurial element, because Mercury is also the inspirer of the work of healing. On the other hand, there is perceptible in the Emmaus story — apart from the Nativity story of the same Luke, the most beautiful New Testament description — the love-bearing beauty of a spirit-pervaded Venus element.)

The appearance to Thomas

This Easter evening has its continuation on the evening of the following Sunday, the first 'octave' of Easter. This time, however, the appearance is meant especially for Thomas, whose doubts therewith melt like snow in the sun. He immediately recognizes the reality and divine sovereignty of the Risen One. The confession of Thomas, 'My Lord and my God' (John 20:28) shines sunlike amidst the Easter stories. Here we are in the region of the *Sun.* As modern research in the history of religion has shown, the expression 'Lord and God' was applied in particular to the sun god. The Caesars impiously claimed the title for themselves. Domitian had himself called *Dominus ac Deus noster,* 'our Lord and God.'

Mary Magdalene's very personal cry from the soul, 'Rabboni — Master' is complemented by Thomas's words a week later in the sunlike realm of the spirit. To the 'Master,' to the glorified human Jesus, is added the recognition of the 'Lord' *(Kyrios)* in his Sun-glory; behind and at the same time above that, the 'God' — the eternal Logos of whom the prologue of John's Gospel says he 'was God.' These words of Thomas signify that the disciples are fully conscious of the rising of the Easter-Sun.

The mountain in Galilee

The appearances on the mountain and by the lake in the 'cosmic' Galilean landscape,* from whose whole nature we may assume to belong to the later part of the forty days, now indicate an even greater dimension. On the mountain in Galilee, Christ reveals himself as one to whom 'all authority in heaven and on earth' is given (Matt.28:18). He turns the attention of the disciples to the whole of humanity. 'Go therefore and make disciples of all nations ...' A human race baptized into the mystery of the Holy Trinity is to arise in place of nations held together by ties of blood and waging wars with each other. The little band of disciples was sent out to undertake the greatest conquest the world ever saw. Immeasurable encouragement and enthusiasm for action flow from the words, 'I am with you always.' The forces and energies of *Mars* are here raised to Christian powers.

The Sea of Galilee

The meal of bread and fish by the lake after the miraculous draft of fish (John 21) is wholly *Jupiter.* The planet of wise priesthood shines upon the sacramental mystery of this meal. Jupiter is also the planet of plenitude, which is so impressively

* See Emil Bock, *The Three Years.*

expressed in the superabundant gift of the catch of fish. (According to old tradition, Jupiter stands in a particularly close relationship to the sign of the 'Fishes.') So, too, the different commissions of Peter and John given afterwards, which settled the question of leadership, bear the signature of the priestly sphere of Jupiter.

Ascension

The last appearance finally passes over into the Ascension. The Risen One now completely merges with the profound and sublime forces of the Father. He does not really go away — the 'I am with you always' still holds good. Rather, he now outgrows and surpasses the disciples' power of vision, and in that sense goes 'out of their sight.'

Saturn was always known as the stern guardian of the entrance to the world of the Father. He is the guide up to the realm of the fixed stars and stands guard before the gate of eternity. Saturnian gravity pervades the story of the Ascension. The Christ refers to the ultimate and sublime mysteries of world destiny hidden in the Father when he answers the disciples' question about the time of restoring the kingdom to Israel. 'It is not for you to know the times or seasons which the Father has fixed by his own authority.' But he promises the Holy Spirit, and the angels who appear speak of a renewed seeing of the Christ in the future when he returns in the clouds of heaven. As with the Galilean appearances where we hear of 'the close of the age' (Matt.28:20) and of John's remaining 'until I come' (John 21:22), the sphere of the initially more personal experience here too broadens to encompass great and universal concerns.

The place of the Ascension, the Mount of Olives, also has something of the threshold-guarding gravity of Saturn. It was on the Mount of Olives, in Gethsemane, that Christ struggled for strength to fulfil the will of the Father right to the end. It is as if the Mount of Olives were always associated with the gravity of facing the final and ultimate. From the Mount of

Olives, the disciples see the Lord enter into the eternal will of the Father.

It seems that through higher inspiration the Gospels 'selected' just these seven Easter stories that so clearly bear the character of the seven planetary stages. We can thus feel that Ascension at the end of forty days is no abrupt and unexpected event, but that it is organically prepared. The Risen One 'grows' within the forty days, the powers of ever fresh supersensible realms stream towards him, he bears the resurrection body deeper and deeper into being, makes it from day to day as it were more 'existent' and more substantial, until in the Ascension he is ready for union with the Father in Heaven. Thus at the beginning of this process the goal is already anticipated when on Easter morning the Risen One says to Mary Magdalene: '... I am ascending to my Father and your Father, to my God and your God' (John 20:17).

8. The miraculous draft of fish

One of the Easter stories in the Gospels is that of the miraculous draft of fish described in the last chapter of John's Gospel. It is worth noting that there is a parallel to it — also a similar story about a draft of fish, but one which takes place not after the Resurrection but much earlier, right at the beginning of Christ's ministry. It is described by Luke (Luke 5:1-11).

Faced with two such closely related accounts modern criticism hastily concludes that we are dealing with the same story: that it is quite obviously a case of one and the same 'legend,' which John places in connection with the Resurrection appearances, while Luke thinks it belongs to the earlier time.

Such a superficial way of looking at it cannot do the Gospel justice. One really has to take time to look at both accounts in quietude in order to see that there are characteristic and significant differences.

The fifth chapter of Luke takes us into the 'Galilean spring' of Christ's work. Christ is staying by the Lake of Gennesaret. He gets into Simon Peter's fishing boat and asks him 'to put out a little from the land.' Thus he speaks from the boat to the multitude thronging on the shore. Then he says to Peter: 'Put out into the deep ...' (literally, according to the Greek), that is, the middle of the lake furthest from the shore where the water is deepest. There they are to cast their nets. Peter says: 'Master, we toiled all night and took nothing! But at your word I will let down the nets.' As a result they make the miraculous catch. He brings them such abundance that the nets break. The other boat has to come up to help save the catch, the boats themselves threaten to sink. Peter falls down before Christ and says: 'Depart from me, for I am a sinful man, O Lord.'

At the time of this catch the Baptism in the Jordan does not lie so far behind. At the Baptism the Christ entered into the body of Jesus of Nazareth, but he has first to take full hold of it and penetrate it. He is still too much a heavenly being to be fully at home in the earthly world. The great 'transformation' of his divine, cosmic powers into the human and terrestrial has only begun; it will only be completed in the earthly death on Golgotha. So far the earthly element is strange to him.

It is not accidental that of the four elements (nowadays one speaks of 'physical states') one bears the name 'earth.' It is as if our planet, Earth, were really only itself within the range of solid elements — as if the other elements, although also found on Earth, do not in the same sense belong to it. In fact the water on Earth is not so thoroughly earthly. It is like the intrusion of a more rarefied kind of existence which is fluid, more versatile and permeating. The liquid element is able to serve on earth as the vehicle for super-earthly life-forces; it is like a visible earthly representation of them.

Christ frequently stays by the lake. As a non-earthly being he feels, as it were, at home and familiar with the element of the sea. It is as if the lake made it easier for him to use his higher powers. When he allows himself to be taken 'a little from the land' by Peter for his sermon, it need not be only a practical measure in order to be able to speak to the multitude from a more favourable position. One could imagine that something of the pressure of physical existence was thereby removed. And now this goes even further: 'Put out into the deep ...' Again one could imagine that with every stroke of the oars away from the shore something of the oppression of being physically incarnated falls from him. Out there, where the influence of the solid earth is least felt, he can become more aware of his innate divine, cosmic being, and unfold its powers. On 'the deep' he reveals to the disciples the hidden richness of the sea.

What the disciples experience there with him is that he is truly a heavenly being who out of inexhaustible abundance is able to offer the gifts of a supersensible world. The great haul of fish — whether it happened physically, which is perfectly conceivable, or was a vision of the disciples in a certain state of excarnation — becomes a pictorial expression of this experience. The disciples have caught nothing during the whole of the previous night. Their nets have remained empty. This becomes a symbol of how man is no longer able to gain anything for his daily existence from the nocturnal immersion of his soul in the sea of supersensible life. He no longer brings from the higher worlds any inspiration for the following day. Christ helped the disciples towards a new and fruitful connection with the supersensible.

Out on the deep water the disciples perceived something of the supra-earthly, heavenly quality of Christ's being, which became perceptible to them as 'quite different' from their dark, burdened, earthly nature, something strange, frightening, judicial. This comes out in Peter's words: 'Depart from me, for I am a sinful man, O Lord.' Such a profound upheaval of the soul could certainly not have been caused by an outer event alone, by an unexpectedly successful catch of fish. The disciples, however, are but imperfectly prepared for the great moment wherein, as if by a lighting up of the cosmic mystery of the Christ, the hidden riches are revealed to them. They can salvage only a part of the catch — '... their nets were breaking ...'. Who does not know on waking that melting away and getting lost of a significant dream, of which one can perhaps bring back only a few scraps into waking consciousness? It is an experience that gives an indication of how we could understand this 'breaking of the nets.'

The other draft of fish after the Resurrection mysteriously mirrors this catch at the time of the beginning in Galilee. An experience that the disciples were privileged to have at the beginning of their discipleship returns. Now, however, it is significantly transformed.

It is also the case with the event described in the last chapter

of John that the disciples have cast their nets in vain the night
before. They have remained empty. Again Christ helps them to
an abundant catch. But this time he is not with them in the
boat. This time he is standing on the beach. They see him there
as the boat nears the shore in the grey light of dawn. He gives
them the advice to cast their nets 'to the right.' As a result
they make the great catch. This time — the evangelist emphasizes it — the net does not break. Peter draws it ashore intact.
There Christ has the early morning meal with them.

This time the catching of fish is connected with an appearance of the Risen One during the forty days between Easter
and Ascension. He appears standing on the shore. From there,
from the land, he works the miracle of the opening of the sea.
We see in this the great change that has come about since the
event of Golgotha. Christ as God of heaven stood first of all
outside the fate of death; he did not by nature, as it were,
know death. Now he has taken it into the sphere of his divine
experience. Thereby he has established kinship with man on
earth, which is necessary if he is to be truly able to communicate with him. Only now after he has been through death,
which is peculiar to man on earth, has he become like one of
us and can really call 'his own,' 'brothers' (John 20:17). The
great transformation is complete; heaven has set foot on earth.
It is from the earth that he now transmits his great power to
the disciples. It is from the earth that he now makes the
supersensible world fruitful for his own so that it yields
nourishing food for the tender spiritual seed in man. It is to
this that Christ appeals in the disciples when he asks them:
'Little children, have you anything to eat?' (John.21:5F).

There is also a connection between this Earth-Mystery of
Golgotha and the Risen One giving advice to cast the net 'to
the right.' On the right side we are more consciously oriented
towards earthly things. The right hand is normally the skillful
one which has the task of taking hold of the substance of the
earth and actively transforming it. When those of ancient times
wanted to make contact with the supersensible world, they

gave themselves up more to the dark dreamlike forces of their soul. At that time this was right. At one time the Lord gave to his own in sleep without their doing anything. Then the net was cast as it were on the left side. Meanwhile man learnt more and more about dealing with the material world and thereby developed and exercised altogether new powers of alertness and self awareness. These powers should not be left outside the sphere of the religious and spiritual. As he goes on developing in our era, man on earth has to learn to transform his alertness, which all too often serves quite unholy, egotistical interests, into something holy. If he does not manage reverently to offer the clear consciousness and presence of mind he has gained to higher worlds, their gifts are less and less able to reach him. The self-awareness that has arisen in the earthly world can be changed into 'selfless selfhood,' and this selfless selfhood is the means of becoming aware of Christ. The powers of the 'right side' are also to be conquered for dealing with the spiritual. It is on these powers that the Risen One calls when he says: 'Cast the net on the right side ...'

Moreover this is connected with the fact that this time the whole catch can be brought ashore. By emphasizing that despite the multitude of large fish 'the net was not torn' (21:11), the evangelist clearly wishes to bring out the difference from that other draft of fish. This time the proceedings are not characterized by failure to cope properly, and by danger (the nets breaking, the ship being in danger of sinking). The full undamaged net is brought in. The increasing of their awareness is also noticeable in the way the disciples gradually come to full recognition of the reality of Christ's presence. At first everything is more like a dream; they do not know who the figure on the shore is (21:4). Then John's words of recognition come like a flash: 'It is the Lord!'* His recognition

---

* Friedrich Rittelmeyer once pointed out how this sentence resounds three times in the account (21:7,12), and how the Greek words *ho Kyrios estin* could at the same time be understood as 'The Lord *is*.'

that they actually had the Risen One before them first spreads to Peter and then to the other disciples as well, although for them it is still at first a strange dreamlike mixture of knowing and not knowing (21:12). But then the Risen One 'comes' (21:13) and takes the meal with them. He 'comes,' he reveals still more forcibly that he is absolutely real; he becomes as it were still more 'existent' for the disciples. And that happens in connection with the sacramental event of the breakfast. In bread and fish the gifts of the earth and sea are linked. Through Christ the earthly, like the heavenly, contributes to the building of the being of man. In the blessed presence of the Risen One Peter, although guilty of his recent denial, no longer speaks as before, 'Depart from me ...' By means of Golgotha and Easter Christ has given sinful men the possibility of transformation. Instead of the tragic 'Depart from me ...' there comes the holy meal, the Communion.

9. The great 'Today' in the New Testament

The idea of experiencing time in three forms — past, present and future — is one that is familiar to us, but we are not always conscious of the fact that grasping the 'present' has its special difficulties. No sooner has something happened than it already belongs to the past, though till now it lay in the future. The present in time is like the point in space — it has no magnitude. If we can grasp it with 'presence' of mind before it has escaped us again, then something higher than the merely temporal is brought into play. Like lightning, eternity flashes in. Eternity is by no means just endlessly prolonged time, but belongs to a quite different and higher plane above and beyond the temporal.

Since there is such a special inbuilt possibility of glimpsing eternity in experiencing the present, words the language has formed for expressing present time, like 'now' and 'today,' can be understood in a deeper religious sense. The mystic knows a *nunc eternam,* an eternal Now. In the Bible the word 'today' frequently has a very special overtone.

From our experience of Christmas there remains with us the sound of the angels' announcement: '... for to you is born this day ... a Savior' (Luke 2:11). In connection with this Christmas Gospel deeply Christian souls have always felt that since Bethlehem 'this day' lives on in Christendom. 'This day' was not only for the shepherds in the fields at that time, for it would long since have become 'yesterday' and 'the day before yesterday'; the mystery of the Saviour's birth wants to come about in every Christian soul anew. In the light of the Christian celebration of Christmas, 'this day' of long ago becomes something present, into which eternity shines straight from heaven.

Once the inner ear has opened for the special sound of the Christmas 'today,' then you also hear it with new overtones and undertones in other places in the Gospels. This is particularly the case with Luke, whose Gospel it is that includes the Christmas story.

If we turn the pages one chapter further in his Gospel, we find the Baptism in the Jordan. If we go back to the original text of Luke still used by Clement of Alexandria and Origen, we find that he gives the words God speaks at the Baptism somewhat differently from Matthew and Mark: 'Thou art my Son, today I have begotten thee' (Luke 3:22). Superficially observed this is a quotation from the Old Testament, from the second Psalm (2:7). But how is it that the voice of God uses just these words? If we look it up, we see that in Psalm 2 it is also God's voice that speaks. On both occasions it is as it were the same voice sounding in heaven, which in Old Testament times came to the ears of the writer of the second Psalm and which at the Baptism was heard by Jesus and John the Baptist. Christ is, as our Creed says, 'the Son born in eternity.' His going forth from the Father is not an occurrence that lies in the past; as an eternal event it belongs to that higher plane that lies above the temporal. In an eternally procreative speaking the Father pronounces his Son, the 'Word.' The second Psalm has caught something of this eternally happening event. It gives the Messiah the words: 'I will declare the decree: the Lord hath said unto me, Thou art my Son; this day have I begotten thee' (AV). The psalmist heard the same as was heard again later at the Baptism in Jordan. With the Baptism the Son born in eternity finally descends into the earthly body of Jesus. The eternal 'Today' thereby shines into an earthly and temporal 'today.'

Soon after, in the fourth chapter, we are met by the third significant 'Today.' Luke records how after the Baptism and Temptation Jesus of Nazareth appears for the first time before men as the Christ. On the sabbath he goes into the synagogue at Nazareth, with which he was well acquainted from his early life, and makes use of the right of adult members to take part in the reading of the scriptures. Luke gives us a clear picture of the preliminaries. 'And he stood up to read' (4:16). The scroll of the prophet Isaiah is handed to him. Providence is at work even in this minor contingency. He opens the scroll and 'finds' the messianic passage, Isaiah 61: 'The Spirit of the Lord is upon me ...' This links up in a wonderful way with his experience at the Baptism. He reads to the point: 'to proclaim the acceptable year of the Lord.' He ends the reading just at the point where in Isaiah it goes on: 'and the day of vengeance ...' There is a divine sovereignty in the way he breaks off at this point. 'He closed the book and gave it back to the attendant' (4:20). Then he sat down in order to add a word of his own to the reading, as a rabbi was permitted to do. The teaching was done sitting down, from the rabbinical chair, but what now comes is something quite different from the discourse of a rabbi. When Christ now speaks for the first time from his own inner being, it is the Word made flesh that begins to speak on earth. Luke's description captures the drama of this unique moment: '... and the eyes of all the synagogue were fixed on him.' What will his first saying be? 'And he began to say to them: "Today this scripture has been fulfilled in your hearing".' But those there are not equal to the historic moment. Full of wonder they readily perceive the 'gracious' quality of his words, but they know no better than to say that this is 'Joseph's son.' They were not able to grasp the great 'Today' in which the angels' message and God's voice at the Baptism still sounded on, wanting to enter their small 'today.' Thus the tragedy of Golgotha already begins.

On a later occasion — after the healing of the paralytic in Capernaum — it seems as if a feeling for this 'Today' of the Christ-day that has dawned begins to stir in the people. They are seized with *ekstasis* in face of the act of healing, which means to a certain extent freed from their everyday, body-bound consciousness, so that in 'awe,' in holy amazement they perceive the divine and cry out: 'We have seen strange things today!' (5:26). It is only Luke's account that so impressively concludes the whole story with the word 'today.'

The thirteenth chapter of Luke describes how Christ on his way to his last Passover receives warning of a possible attack by Herod. 'Behold, I cast out demons and perform cures today and tomorrow, and the third day I finish my course. Nevertheless I must go on my way today and tomorrow and the day following; for it cannot be that a prophet should perish away from Jerusalem.' (13:32f). Christ is aware of his destiny: it is not yet, but soon; it will not be here in Galilee, but in Jerusalem. His allotted time on earth approaches its end. The God who has become man humbly accommodates himself to the pattern of events in time on earth. He feels how precious is the short span of fleeting time yet granted him, which he fills with everlasting deeds of love. The 'today' of time and space still applies to him; he knows that it can still continue into a 'tomorrow,' but then will be the day for the final deed of fulfilment. He walks towards it. This 'today,' overshadowed by the approaching Passion, is a powerfully striking expression of Christ's feeling about the dwindling number of days allotted him on earth.

In the story of the Passion Luke — this time together with Mark — has the word 'today' in the pronouncement of Peter's denial: '... the cock will not crow this day ...' (22:34). It is the crowing of the cock that announces the dawning of the day of Golgotha. The word 'today' is spoken yet a second time on Good Friday, and again recorded only in Luke's account. Here on the last occasion it is once more the tremendous 'Today' into which the light of eternity streams in full brilliance. It is Christ's saying from the cross: 'Truly, I say to you, today you will be with me in Paradise' (23:43). The criminal on his cross experiences in the last hour of his fast dwindling life on earth how for him 'is born this day' the Saviour. The end and the beginning of the Gospel are thus linked. Luke is therefore in a special sense the evangelist of 'Today.'

We must, however, draw on Matthew to supplement this in

relation to the Lord's Prayer; for he alone (not Luke, if we keep to the original text) passes on the prayer that daily bread may 'this day' be given us. This speaks of the inner superiority over all anxiety in the future. But such a superiority can exist only if each day is experienced as belonging to God, if, that is, the great 'Today' of eternity shines into the temporal. (In the other place where Matthew uses the word 'today' its significance does not go beyond the usual use of the word and need not therefore be mentioned in our connection.)

'Today' once more plays a special role in the New Testament in the Letter to the Hebrews. The author, well-versed in the scriptures, quotes the ninety-fifth Psalm. As with the second Psalm, when we read it we notice the sound of divine inspiration. The soul of the psalmist is moved by what has gone before and is made receptive for listening to an inspiration from the highest realm. 'Today if ye will hear his voice, Harden not your heart' (Ps.95:7f). He looks back to the fate of Israel wandering in the wilderness when the people fell into hardness and bitterness of heart and therefore could not find the way to rest in the promised land. The psalmist feels himself at a turning point in history when again — as in the time of Moses — God's voice calls to men. Again, as before, there arises as a result a 'Today' pregnant with destiny. The New Testament Letter to the Hebrews goes back to this word and gives it current significance. It expresses the conviction that the full truth and decisive significance of this 95th Psalm which God spoke 'through David' (Heb.4:7) is manifest only after the Christ event. Only we Christians are fully able to understand it. Three times it is solemnly quoted: 'Today, when you hear his voice, do not harden your hearts' (Heb.3:7f,15; 4:7). Without prejudice to its historical reality, the fate of Israel — exodus from Egypt, journeying in the wilderness, entry into the promised land — appears as a prototypal event in which a yet greater has already taken shape. After the loss of the old spirituality the whole of humanity has entered the desert and is to find the promised land of the new covenant with God. So for the Letter to the Hebrews the full significance of what was recorded in the Old Testament was not exhausted with the events of those times. A new desert wandering is in process on an enormous scale. God has called forth a new day of salvation with a new 'horizon,' a new 'Today' (Heb.4:7). It concerns the hearing of the voice, the dawning of eternity in the consciousness of Christians so that the way can be found into the promised land. The Letter to the Hebrews seeks to bring about an apocalyptic awakening with this 'Today.'

We can make it our own in this present era. It has meanwhile again become 'much truer.' Even the soul experiences connected with the desert wandering, which the Letter to the Hebrews describes as hardening of heart, we can see in a wholly modern light. '... do not harden your hearts as in the rebellion' (3:15). Only the grasping of the presence of Christ in the present time of our twentieth century, only the raising of the ordinary 'today' to the great 'Today' of the breaking in of eternity, can save us.

10. Father of Lights

The Christmas Mood in the Letter of James

There is a verse in the Letter of James that radiates the glory of Christmas and makes an indelible impression on our souls: 'Every good gift and every perfect gift is from above, and cometh down from the Father of lights ...' (Jam.1:17 AV).

These words express the mystery of giving and making gifts. During the Christmas season we can make it our concern to meditate on this mystery. When someone makes a gift, he has the feeling that it cannot just be handed over as it is; he wraps it up, perhaps, in festive looking Christmas paper. This wrapping up is nothing more than a symbol that we ourselves have to turn into reality. The wrapping that really lifts the gift above the 'bare' thing is invisible, and has to be contributed from our souls. It is like an ethereal substance of the soul itself. But it is always at our disposal when we want to make a gift. Where can we find this strength? Whence does it come? James's verse gives the significant answer: 'from above'! The donor must make himself open if something is to flow in from a higher world and bless his giving. If you have realized that, then you may with good conscience tell a child that the gift comes from Father Christmas; it is the deeper truth in comparison with the trivial fact that you have perhaps bought the present in a shop.

The gift from above is the Christ-child. Every true gift is related to this original Christmas gift. The Greek text of James's letter uses the word 'descend' *(katabainō),* the same word that is so often used of Christ in the Gospel of John. Every good gift descends from above. Translating literally, one should say 'is descending' (Latin, *descedens)* — a continuously happening event, a permanent Christmas.

By careful consideration of the Greek words we can come still closer to James's text than is possible by means of the well known Authorized Version. This twice translates 'gift' — 'every good gift and every perfect gift' — which blurs a fine distinction in the original text. There first of all it says *dósis;* the second time *dōrēma.* The different endings of the Greek words show that with *dósis* the action of giving is emphasized, whilst *dōrēma* on the other hand is what is given, the gift received. (RSV translates: 'Every good endowment and every perfect gift is from above ...')

Correspondingly, the related adjectives are also different. The 'endowment' is 'good,' the 'gift' 'perfect.' 'Good' is a word for the highest, applicable to the very Godhead. For Plato the idea of goodness is the sun in the realm of ideas. 'No one is good but God alone' we read in the Gospel. The 'good' endowment is therefore a giving from the primary divine source. Just as 'good' indicates the primary source of all creation, so 'perfect' *(teleios)* indicates the final goal, the future perfection. The 'perfect gift' is called perfect not only in view of its faultlessness, but also because it helps the recipient to become perfect. It does not mean for him an additional burden to those he already bears through life, but it promotes his development, brings him further on his way.

One could paraphrase the Greek text thus: 'Every act of giving from the primary source of good, and every gift that helps the recipient towards perfection — is descending from above.'

But that is not the end of the verse. As the inner experience moves on, the 'above' turns into a sublime vision of divine being: '... from above, *from the Father of lights.*' This plural, 'lights,' refers to the stars. We can see from Paul's First Letter to the Corinthians how the stars were once still felt to be living beings. He speaks of every star shining in a way peculiar to itself. Man still knew that the shining of the stars — in the same way as the light coming forth from the eyes of men — is the outer manifestation of some inner quality behind them.

63

Man saw in the fullness of the stars the visible sign of a fullness of spirits, of the heavenly hosts.

As late as the thirteenth century the works of Dionysius the Areopagite enjoyed the greatest veneration. In them ancient wisdom lived on: not only below men are the kingdoms ranged in descending order to the mineral, but above them the ladder continues on up into the invisible. Above men are the angels, above these the archangels, and so through three times three ordered hierarchies right up to the exalted seraphim who glow with holy love before the countenance of God. The book, *Celestial Hierarchies,* in which Dionysius the Areopagite deals with the nine angelic realms, solemnly begins with this verse of James, and puts the phrase about the Father of lights as a motto for the whole work.

The verse makes the further step of distinguishing between the world of lights and the Father God himself who, as Schiller says, 'dwells above the tent of stars.' The starry heaven appears to comprise manifold movements. There is rising and setting, there are turning points between ascending and descending, there is moving and changing. Exalted above all this variability is the Father. He is bearer and guarantor of what remains the same and keeps its own identity through all change. All change, that is to say, also presupposes such a principle of the 'constant.' Otherwise everything would lose itself in continually becoming something else. How different is the old man from the child he once was, and yet through the changes there runs a permanence that preserves the 'sameness' of the person. This all-pervading permanence is ultimately embodied in the Father God himself, of whom the James verse further says: 'with whom there is no variation or shadow due to change' (RSV) or 'with whom there is no variation and no being shaded as a result of the turning of the stars *[aposkiasma tropēs]' (F).*

The calm constancy of the Father does not, however, necessarily imply a dogma of immoveable rigidity whereby God would cease to be the 'living God.' From the calm of his exalted realm above the stars the all-loving Father bends down and sends the earth his Son. The verse immediately following that about 'the Father of lights' pronounces very explicitly the mystery of Christ's birth. 'Of his own will begat he us with the word of truth, that we should be a kind of first fruits of his creatures' (1:18 AV).

In the Greek text, however, we do not find the verb 'to beget,' but a word that apart from the Letter of James does not appear in the whole New Testament: *apekuēsen*. The image is not taken from that of male begetting, but from that of motherhood. What is meant is the bringing forth of a being that was previously formed in the womb and now by birth is released into its own independent existence. The Father of lights has given humanity birth — in this image, the Letter of James pronounces the mystery of Christianity.

Originally man — or what was to become man — was still completely contained within the upper worlds of light like the unborn child in the womb, still carried and protected. He was gradually released from this divine, cosmic womb for his own independent existence on the earth. But, as he has walked the earth till now, man is still incomplete. He is not yet completely born. He always gives the impression of unsatisfactoriness, often appearing to be quite godless and godforsaken. 'What we are here, a god can there complete,' says a perceptive late poem of Hölderlin. He had a feeling for the fact that man needs his nature completing from above. Christianity, however, knows that this completion not only awaits us 'there,' but that it is gradually to permeate us already 'here' on earth. For through Christ's descending to earth the completion from above has come within our reach as the gift that leads us to perfection. Through Christ's becoming man the higher part of our being has stepped forth from the womb of heaven, has in him for the first time been brought forth into earthly human form. In Christ Jesus humanity as a whole has for the first time reached the point of being born. It is therefore now a question of this Christ birth also coming about in us as individuals. But in principle the Letter of James is right in saying: '... he brought us forth ...'. The actual name of Christ is not here used, but the connection with Christ is given by the addition: 'by the word of truth,' for this word, the Logos, has appeared in Christ. Through the Logos of truth our higher nature, formerly hidden in the womb of heaven, is born into our human nature on earth and is thereby given to us.

The phrase introducing this sentence we have not yet considered. 'Of his own will ...' Translated literally: 'having willed it.' *Voluntarie* — 'willingly' — is the Latin translation. 'Having willed it, he brought us forth.' The Greek used here for 'will' — Greek has more than *one* word for it — has the same stem as the noun *boulē*, which means 'decision.' A willing is therefore meant that proceeds from a foregoing decision. Allowing man to come forth, with all the risk involved in a nature destined for freedom but also open to seduction, necessitated a unique decision of the Deity, in which is included from the very beginning the readiness for sacrifice on the cross. Therefore in Christ was seen the 'messenger of the great decision.' The biblical phrase stumblingly signifies in the insufficient language of men proceedings of the most exalted nature within the Godhead: 'having willed it' — 'of his own will.'

Regarded in the light of evolution man is the highest achievement of the earth's development. His appearance concluded the creation. The birth of Christ, however, means that the last to appear, the 'lastborn,' becomes the 'firstborn' of a world which is renewed by men permeated by Christ, and in which also all creatures are to be redeemed and transformed. On man's salvation or lack of it depends salvation or lack of it for the kingdoms of nature below him. 'From his own resolve he had the will and brought us forth from the womb of heaven by the Word of truth, that we should be the firstborn of his whole creation.'

11. Christianity's potential for the future
The third chapter of the Letter to the Philippians

The true nature of Christianity is misunderstood by many people, which means that it is generally accepted that being a Christian entails weak passivity and an outlook oriented toward the past. If one traces Christianity to its sources, one finds something quite different. The third chapter of the Letter to the Philippians, for example, is a classic expression of the future potential, of the 'dynamic' of the Christian frame of mind.

Paul speaks there first of all of what had been important for him in earlier years, but how then through his encounter with Christ a revaluation of all values, a complete change and refounding of his whole attitude to life came about. What was previously significant for him fades before the 'surpassing worth of knowing Christ Jesus my Lord' (Phil.3:8). In our times when church theologians so often play off 'faith' against 'knowledge,' it is really a relief to see how unaffectedly and as a matter of course Paul speaks here of knowledge, and how for him knowledge *(gnōsis)* and faith *(pistis)* do not exclude one another but work harmoniously together. Without knowing Christ faith would not be possible, as Paul says on one occasion in the Second Letter to Timothy (1:12). 'I know whom I have believed.' The offering of the heart in faith to what is known leads on to a deepening of knowledge — thus knowledge and faith increase together.

The 'surpassing worth of knowing Christ Jesus' leads to faith in him who gives men true righteousness (3:9). This righteousness 'which is through faith,' so particularly stressed by Paul, is in no way a remote theological dogma but a truth which is more relevant today than ever. If we want to express it in modern words, we could perhaps say: Man comes ever closer to crisis in his human condition. The highly developed intelligence that triumphs in technology and a moral immaturity completely disproportionate to this cleverness are in stark opposition within him. Man is on the way to becoming a terrible menace in the life of the world. What he contributes to existence cannot equal what the divine powers of creation have as it were 'invested' in him. The scales are not evenly balanced. According to higher justice man's right to existence in the universe would really have to be denied him; he seems to be something of a failure, a divine 'bad investment.' This negative way of judging our humanity is very much in the air these days. A great deal of the nihilism and the cynicism that fills the lives of our contemporaries comes fundamentally from such conscious or unconscious despair about humanity. One cannot, however, finally judge of the justification for man's existence if one does not take into account that since the time of Golgotha the divine being of Christ has thrown himself into the scales on humanity's side. He has joined himself with the fate of humanity. Everything now depends on whether men become aware of this fact and the infinite encouragement and hope it gives, and from their side unite themselves with Christ to say with Paul they 'believe in him.' From such a turning towards Christ there begins to grow in men the seed of a more exalted humanity in the future. Christ thus becomes the guarantor of our true future. If we cling to him, he carries us over the abyss of feeling that we have no right to exist. We can therefore be justified before the divine justice not by looking at what we have achieved hitherto, but rather by looking at the seedlike beginning of the permeation of our being by Christ, which is possible since the sacrificial deed on Golgotha. In this sense Paul speaks of the righteousness from God which has come to him by faith in Christ (3:9).

This experience of faith now leads on to an enhanced knowledge. Following on directly from Paul's words justifying faith, there are others that emanate from such faith: '... that I may know him and the power *[dynamis]* of his resurrection, and may share his sufferings ...' (3:10). This knowledge is set out in a threefold way. First of all knowledge of 'him.' But one cannot possibly know 'him' in his true nature without immediately becoming aware of the power that emanates from this being, and which cannot be separated from him — the power of conquering death. 'The power of his resurrection' is as it were the first decisive and characteristic impression of the Christ-Being that one receives. Thirdly, there follows what is received from the knowledge deepened by faith: 'and may share his sufferings.' How does this third element intrinsically connect with what goes before?

For one who knows 'him' and 'the power of his resurrection' the question then arises how to make 'him' and his 'power' one's own in the sense that Paul uses the expression, 'gain Christ.' Knowledge has the answer to this: this 'gaining' can happen only on the path of true sympathy with Christ. 'Sym-pathy,' that is, 'suffering with.' If you look at Christ with an open mind as he goes through his fate on Golgotha, you gradually come to feel this suffering with him, even finally to be drawn into it yourself — right to the point of experiencing 'being crucified with Christ' as Paul says in another place. You cannot attain the power of his resurrection if you wish to avoid such suffering.

On the cross Christ certainly took upon himself humanity's burden of sin. To do such a thing was possible only for a divine being; no one else would have been able even to lift this terrible load under which humanity would surely have succumbed. But Christ's deed of redemption can bear fruit only if man is willing to help carry his poor and modest share of the burden carried by Christ. Paul says in the Letter to the Colossians (1:24) that he suffered what Christ, as it were, had left to be suffered. It is part of this mystery of redemption that man does not receive it absolutely passively, but that he is himself considered worthy of sharing in fulfilment of his own redemption and that of the whole of humanity. The divine help that comes to us in Christ does not make our individual effort superfluous but works in with it. The Christian is not to be relieved of all suffering. He is rather to become acquainted with suffering of a higher grade — and is privileged to do so. He may himself share in God's suffering for humanity. So, after he has felt the breath of resurrection emanating from Christ, there comes to Paul the profound knowledge of the 'communion with his suffering' now open to man. It leads him on to a personal experience of sharing in the death undergone on Golgotha. Thereby he experiences an inner transformation laying hold of his whole being — *symmorphizómenos,* that is, 'in a similar form' to his death *(morphē,* form).

From the depths of such suffering-with, dying-with, there now emerges the possibility of personally gaining the 'power of his resurrection.' Paul, however, speaks of this with all timidity and restraint, with a cautious, tentative 'if possible.' '... that if possible I may attain the resurrection from the dead' (Phil.3:11).

He sees a mighty though far-distant goal ahead of him, before whose awe-inspiring greatness he feels a deep modesty: 'Not that I have already attained this or am already perfect' (3:12). He is conscious of the fact that he stands within a long-term process of becoming. Paul also speaks in the Second Letter to the Corinthians of such a gradual progress in inner development when he writes about changing into the Lord's likeness 'from one degree of glory to another' (2Cor.3:18).

'Not that I have already attained this or am already perfect: *but I press on to make it my own ...'* And again we find that feeling-of-the-way towards future possibility which could be translated: *'If perhaps I may lay hold of it* because I am laid hold of by Christ Jesus' (Phil.3:12).

Man is deemed worthy of partnership by God, his free will not excluded. God does not wish all the activity to be on his side; he wants man to work with him. Being 'taken hold of' by Christ comes first. But this must be followed by the active 'taking hold' by man. An example may explain this. You hear a symphony and are 'taken' by it. If however you are more profoundly interested and really want to make the symphony 'your own,' then you will procure the score and work on it until you can fully grasp that by which you were so 'taken.' It is the same with shaking hands. It is not enough if someone who wants to greet me grasps my hand; I must make a similar gesture on my side.

Paul's modesty is again expressed: 'Brethren, I do not consider that I have made it my own.' But to one thing he may lay claim for himself: 'but one thing I do, forgetting what lies behind and straining forward to what lies ahead' (3:13). He feels like a competitor in the ancient games, having only the goal and the victor's prize before his eyes (3:14). In a unique manner these words manifest the forceful, forward-looking nature of the Christian attitude.

'Forgetting what lies behind.' Perhaps it is not superfluous in these times of ours to dwell a little on this statement and make clear in more detail what it says — and what it does not say. It could possibly be understood as a confirmation of that mood so widespread today of wanting to jettison all reflection on the past as troublesome ballast, and to live quite simply for the day. Any feeling for remembrance has got lost in this giddy-paced age. The coherence, the continuity of life is in danger of becoming lost, existence is in danger of falling into disconnected, isolated moments. Paul's words about the great forgetting certainly have nothing to do with this. Other remarks of the apostle show clearly enough how important to him was the connection with the past. Even in his wording of the account of the Last Supper we find the word 'remembrance' in connection with both bread and wine (1Cor.11:24f). It is the consideration of the Christian celebration of the Last Supper in particular that gives us an important clue as to the Christian experience of time and its three dimensions. The three years from the Baptism to Golgotha belong historically to the past. The remembrance of the events in Palestine is entrusted to the memory of humanity as something that may never be forgotten. Should the remembrance of these events disappear completely from humanity's consciousness, it would face a catastrophe that would correspond — but on a large scale — to the pathological loss of individual personal retrospection. Insofar as it is a 'remembrance' it is first of all the concern of the celebration of the Last Supper to maintain the connection with Christ's deed. But it is just when this remembrance is truly observed that Christ's deed proves not merely to belong to the past. It is not confined within the bounds of merely having been; it breaks through these bounds and proves that it works on in the present. The living Christ is experienced as the Present One. The remembrance of the 'then' enables us to do justice to the present, truly be 'up to date' with our times. If we disregard the words that he is 'with us always,' we allow the fulness of the present to escape us. And then this rich present, too, breaks its bounds and opens towards the future. The Christ who becomes present in the Communion Service reveals himself as the One who is to come. He comes towards us and offers us our own future. Each time we receive Communion, the growth of the future man in us is fostered. Christianity as it presents itself in the sacrament of the body and blood of Christ comprises true remembering, real present, and therefore also genuine future. In contrast there is the opposite picture threatening humanity: the lost connection with the past, the thoughtless living-for-the-day, the anxiety for what is coming.

'Forgetting what lies behind' also certainly does not mean that we should simply let yesterday remain undigested and not deal with it properly. In that case we should not get free from it. Anyone who does not develop a right attitude toward the past is, as experience shows, all the more helplessly abandoned to all the possible ill consequences of a past event. The soul then gets 'hooked' to this and that, very often quite unconsciously; it cannot 'get over it.' If you look back as a Christian, then wrongs done to others in the past can be taken hold of by the transforming forces of Christ's forgiveness. The consequences of the deed are then borne with a soul at peace, the remembrance is certainly painful but is no longer 'galling.' The pain becomes fruitful in that it now proves to be even more of an incentive to do good. Similarly the memory of the wrong that was inflicted on you by another, the gnawing and poisoning of the soul, also fades if you know how very much you are in need of forgiveness yourself, and if it is clear to you that you cannot be a partaker of forgiveness if you are not willing to put it into action yourself. Or if it is not a case of right and wrong but of the blows of fate, of an irrecoverably lost fortune, of horror and terror that is experienced, even that takes on a different character if it is digested in submission to the wise and ultimately good-intentioned powers of destiny. It is when we take care to remember in the right way that the loved one who has died increasingly becomes like one present who moves on into a higher world, and who remains connected with us in all that is highest and best. Then we overcome what keeps the soul fettered in unfruitfully looking back to the pain, separation and sense of deprivation we have already undergone. Thus we can understand Paul's saying about 'forgetting' as a dismissal of what monopolizes the soul from the past in what one might call an unlawful manner, what makes it insensitive for the demands of our times, and shuts it off from the possibilities that press towards it from the future. '... forgetting what lies behind and straining forward to what lies ahead ...'.

12. The seven Beatitudes of the Apocalypse

A Path towards Resurrection

Less well known than the beatitudes of the Sermon on the Mount, but not less significant, are the seven that are found in various places throughout the Revelation of John. They shine all the brighter against the background of apocalyptic catastrophes. According to St Augustine the history of Christianity takes its course between the persecutions of the opposing forces and the consolations of God. In this sense, as 'consolations of God,' these beatitudes can shine out to us like bright stars.

— *1* —

Blessed is he who reads aloud the words of the prophecy and blessed are those who hear, and who keep what is written therein; for the time is near (1:3).

This beatitude occurs right at the beginning of the Apocalypse. — The Greek word for 'read' *(anaginōskein)* actually means something like 'know upwards.' What appears in the book is the 'sediment' of an original live experience; it is now relegated to the 'dead letter,' it is 'written down.' But the one who reads with real understanding brings it to life again. His perception rises 'above' what is written 'down.'

To this enlivening act of spiritual perception is added the full, feeling response of the 'listening' soul that relates itself in devotion to the word of the spirit; to this in turn is added the 'sustained will' in 'preserving' or 'keeping.' The original text means by that a sort of garden-tending activity, performed regularly, over and over again. Repetition and regularity are indispensible elements of all spiritual life; it is not for nothing that we speak of 'religious practice.'

Perceptive reading, devoted listening of the soul, consequent action through the regular exercise of the will — with these the Apocalypse in its opening lays the basis of a development that finally leads to participation in the resurrection world of the 'heavenly Jerusalem.'

'Words of the prophecy' are all the words of wisdom that have flowed from a true revelation of Christ. In contrast to pre-Christian wisdom all Christian knowledge is directed toward the future, is apocalyptic, is prophecy.

'For the time is near' does not refer to the indifferent flowing on of time through the hour-glass, *chronos,* but *kairos,* the moment heavy with destiny, charged with decision. With Christ the kingdom of heaven has drawn 'near.' When the soul awakes to this nearness, when it becomes aware of what is brought within its reach, then the decisive hour strikes for it. This moment is 'near' for each one who takes to the path of which the first beatitude of the Apocalypse speaks.

— *II* —

We now have to wait a long time in reading the Revelation of John until the second beatitude appears. What was contained in the first has to last a long time, for there follows the description of catastrophic events, and the Antichrist sets up his rule. Then at last the fourteenth chapter presents the Christ returning in the clouds. Immediately before, as if already in the light of this coming on the 'white cloud,' stands the second beatitude:

> 'Blessed are the dead who die in the Lord henceforth.'
> 'Blessed indeed,' says the Spirit, 'that they may rest
> from their labours, for their deeds follow them!'
> (14:13).

'Blessed are the dead' — a great contrast to the mood of the ancient Greeks who saw the life of the dead in Hades diminished to a grey shadow-like existence. Blessed are the dead — nor is this meant in the pessimistically resigned sense of a materialistic age, which envies the dead because they have fortunately left it 'behind them' and have entered into the 'great nothing.' The Apocalypse is conscious of saying something new in this blessing of the dead, something that first becomes real through Christ, and therefore continues 'from now on' or 'henceforth.' It does not simply bless the dead indiscriminately, but makes the important qualification: 'who die in the Lord.'

The 'rest' they are to find after their great labours certainly does not mean rest in the churchyard, but a profound recovery in the spirit.

What man has done during his existence on earth with all its pain and difficulties, what as an apparently transitory being he has put forth there as transitory deeds in a transitory world — is now revealed in its eternal significance. 'Their deeds follow them.' These real, present consequences of their deeds working on into the supersensible are for the dead a stern judgment. Only those who 'die in Christ' need not fear these consequences.

John then beholds the one who comes on the white cloud with the sickle in his hand. Death has become as it were subservient to Christ as the Lord of destiny.

'Dying in the Lord' is not confined simply to the moment of death. If it is to come about, then it must already have begun during life as an inner 'mystical' process in a soul united with Christ, as a constant sacrifice of the lower self. Paul said: 'I die every day!' and said it, moreover, in his chapter on the Resurrection (1Cor.15:31).

The perceiving, hearing and practice of the first beatitude has to deepen into a 'dying in Christ'; then it leads to the mystery of the one who comes again, of the one who comes on the white cloud.

— III —

> Lo, I am coming like a thief! Blessed is he who is
> awake, keeping his garments that he may not go naked
> and be seen exposed. (16:15).

Christ's coming again, which makes itself felt more and more
as a spiritual fact, asks of man grave decisions. It does not
leave him as he was before. If he sleeps through the event, he
is inwardly the poorer — this is the point of comparison in the
strange and yet realistic picture of Christ coming 'like a thief.'
In comparison with this is the blessing of him who 'is awake.'

In ancient times the Lord gave to his own in sleep, but man
has stepped out of the divine dream of the early childhood of
humanity; he has begun to wake up — primarily at first to the
earthly world. If the wakefulness is limited to the material
world, however, there gradually arises the feeling: 'Unfortunate
are the wakeful.' Man bears this adult awakeness like a burden,
seeks narcotics and opiates in order to escape the desolate
reality. Rightly understood Christianity is not 'opium.' It
means raising the power of wakefulness beyond the material
world into the spiritual. Whoever shrinks back from the full
adult responsibility of sober awakening in order not to 'lose
his childhood faith' does not yet know that all waking and
knowing that could be dangerous to Christianity is always only
a half-waking and half-knowing. It is precisely within the
meaning of Christianity to penetrate to the full awareness and
the full knowledge that includes the supersensible. Therefore,
'Blessed is he who is awake.'

'Keeping his garments.' Everyone knows the sort of dream
in which he finds himself not properly dressed. This can reflect
deeper things. Man is a being with a central core surrounded
by various sheaths. Besides the physical body we carry still
finer supersensible sheaths about us which can be represented
as garments, as in fact they are in the priest's vestments. If
man is not awake, does not 'pull himself together' with all his

ego-core's energy for full awareness, then the sheaths can become estranged from their own centre, and evil things can make their abode in them. If for example we do automatically, indifferently, what we should be doing with our whole being, we allow our sheaths to act independently of us. The same is true if we lack self-control and allow ourselves to be pulled in all directions by our emotions. 'He who is awake' should permeate all the members of his human nature from his inner core outwards — then he 'keeps his garments together.'

Being 'seen exposed' occurs when the man without sheaths permeated by spirit and soul, without the 'cloak of Christian love for his neighbour,' without the aura of his true spiritual nature, represents himself only as a material body, when, to put it crudely, he regards himself and others only as 'so many pounds live weight.' Then the depths of human shame are reached.

He however who keeps his garments also becomes a wearer of the 'wedding garment.'

— IV —

Blessed are those who are invited to the wedding supper of the Lamb' (19:9).

Invited, called by name. The true inner being of man, his individuality, which makes him something unique, unchangeable, irreplaceable, is called upon in the 'name.' Yet our earthly name holds the place of our hidden, eternal name with which God called us into existence. If man hears this eternal name called as by God, then he knows he is invited to the wedding feast of the Lamb. It is in the image of the 'Lamb' that the Christ appears for John as the fulfiller of the great sacrifice of redemption. From the sacrifice of Christ there blossoms forth the great wedding, the marriage of heaven and earth in glorious transformation. In this holy event seen in the image of the 'meal' and the 'marriage' — 'the wedding supper' — the Christian who is fully awake is to share.

— V —

Towards the end of the Apocalypse the beatitudes follow one
another more closely. The calling to the wedding now becomes
an actual 'being chosen.'

> Blessed and holy is he who shares in the first resurrec-
> tion! Over such the second death has no power, but
> they shall be priests of God and of Christ, and they
> shall reign with him a thousand years (20:6).

The word 'holy' is now included in the form of the blessing. He who shares in the wedding feast increases in saint-
liness.

Being able to share in the 'first resurrection' — 'dying in
the Lord' was the precondition for this. What is the 'first'
resurrection? The writer of the apocalypse also distinguishes
between a first and a second death. Neither death nor resurrection can therefore be grasped in a single concept; they are
processes, developments that gradually unfold. The 'first death'
is obviously the death of the earthly body. The 'second death'
is undergone when it becomes clear after the death of the body
that the soul has lost its spiritual home through the way it has
conducted its earthly existence.

Conversely, the 'first resurrection' is the awakening of the
soul that has 'died in the Lord' and is therefore not affected by
the second, the soul death. In the wedding garment of the
higher, Christ-permeated sheaths, it is able to lead a conscious
life after death, in which it can serve Christ as a priest. It lives
like a king in that, with death, it has not had to lay aside the
crown of consciously directed will. It can carry over into life
after death the individual power of the awakened higher ego.
The first 'resurrection' happens therefore in the realm of the
soul and the more subtle life-forces. It does not yet reach the
earthly body so strongly that it can wrest it from the fate of
death, spiritualize it and incorporate it into the higher world —
that would then be the 'second resurrection' that deals with the

'first death,' just as the first resurrection, the inner awakening, renders powerless the second death, the death of the soul. The first resurrection remains in the realm of Holy Saturday when the body still lies in the grave, but when as a radiant soul Christ already brings the light of Easter to the departed souls. When the Church speaks of the 'saints,' strictly speaking it means not only those in the official calendar of saints, but all the Christ-imbued souls that by virtue of the first resurrection reign with Christ in the invisible world like priests and kings.

In the 'thousand years' this working with Christ in the supersensible world gradually matures towards the 'second resurrection' which then also includes the earthly body and overcomes the last enemy, death. This is described in the Apocalypse as the 'heavenly Jerusalem.' In the sphere of this mighty closing picture the penultimate beatitude already confronts us.

— VI —

And behold, I am coming soon. Blessed is he who
keeps the words of the prophecy of this book. (22:7).

Once the first difficulties are overcome, the stream of redeeming events rushes on with full force. The coming of Christ makes itself felt ever more powerfully.

Like the first beatitude this one again speaks of 'keeping,' tending Christianity's wisdom like a gardener for the future. This reference back to the beginning shortly before the end is a reminder that that beginning is not something suspended and set aside by the following stages, but that in principle it already contains the true 'keeping' that leads to perfection. The 'sustained will' of this tending and practice is recognizable in it. The constantly practised enlivening of Christianity's future potential finally reaches its goal.

Separated by only a few verses from the almost disappointingly simple sixth beatitude, which apparently leads so little further, there now follows the seventh and last, which contains the whole Easter mystery of the Resurrection.

— *VII* —

Blessed are those who wash their robes, that they may have the right to the tree of life and that they may enter the city by the gates. (22:14).

'Keeping' the garments was spoken of earlier, now 'washing' them. In the life of the first resurrection there occurs a continuous cleansing of the human being from the stains and blemishes of the Fall. In his earlier vision of all the saints John describes the truly Christian dead as 'clothed in white robes.' '... they have washed their robes and made them white in the blood of the Lamb' (7:14). Their original purity cannot be given again to men except through the power of the great loving sacrifice emanating from Golgotha — 'the blood of the Lamb.' But man must really take hold of this grace, he must 'wash' his 'robe' and make it 'white' in the sacrificial blood. It is surely in reality an added grace that he may co-operate in this. By such working of the effects of Golgotha into the finer sheaths of man's being the 'second' resurrection also becomes possible, the resurrection that finally wrests the earthly body, too, from the forces of death. Those redeemed 'have the right to the tree of life.' The Fall with its consequences is overcome. Fallen man had once to be barred from approaching the tree of life '... lest he put forth his hand ... and live for ever'; he had to be preserved from having to live eternally in his fallen state, estranged from God. Making the sinner subject to death was the greatest boon of Providence. Only through Christ is man gradually to become mature enough to immortalize his true being, restored and perfected in all its members. Once it was said: '... lest he eat'; so now it is said of the purified: '... that they may have the right to the tree of life.' Now man may consciously take up those mysterious, hidden, divine life-forces that no longer allow death its power.

To the picture of the garden of Paradise is added that of the 'city,' the resurrection world of which those who are Christ-imbued are to be the rightful inhabitants.

Whilst the first beatitude contained the motif of 'perception' in the word 'read' *(anaginōskō),* the last contains that of 'life.'

If one looks at these seven beatitudes as a whole, it is also noticeable how singular and plural alternate in them. 'He who reads — those who hear — the dead — he who is awake — those who are invited — he who shares in the first resurrection — they shall be priests — he who keeps the words — those who wash their robes.' It is like a rhythmical breathing in and out, a contraction to the realm of the purely individual and then an expansion again into the element of a higher spirit of community that arises from it, a rhythm of 'I' and 'we.' It begins with the singular of the one who concerns himself with knowing the holy book. It ends with the great 'we' of a future humanity — those who 'have the right to the tree of life' and 'may enter the city by the gates.'

13. Life after death and the Bible

Having a philosophy of life is not a 'luxury' to which we treat ourselves as something apart from the practical demands of life. When someone we love dies, the way in which we adapt ourselves and behave in relation to him is an important part of life's experience, depending very much, however, on our particular view of life. If we are of the opinion that death is the end of everything, then we will behave in quite another way than if we are convinced that the soul lives on. In the first case we shall leave it at nostalgic recollection. We have then, as we think, only to do with our own soul and its emotions, and that no longer concerns the one who has died for he has ceased to exist. In the other case a systematic care in thinking about the dead will have an objective significance beyond our own feelings. We are then not alone with our own soul, but we feel with a certain responsibility that our inner emotions reach the one who has died, could be burdensome to him — or helpful if we do the right thing. On the basis of such a view of life we have begun in The Christian Community to build up something like a 'culture' of relations with the dead in connection with the sacramental life.

We are accustomed to the fact that materialism, where it is represented as a conscious philosophy, lets man's existence end with his bodily existence. But we must regard as alarming the fact that for some time now certain influential streams of Protestant theology also take this point of view. Thus even in such circles, which certainly want to adhere to Christianity, the way is prepared for the materialistic view of man's nature and the consequences for his life. Various theological trends, in other respects not at all united, today coincide in the doctrine that all is over for the soul at death — until the Last Day.

In contrast to atheistical materialism the existence of God is adhered to, but this God and his act of awakening the dead on the Last Day is quite incongruous with the otherwise accepted materialistic outlook. The idea of a soul continuing to exist after death without a physical body is rejected as 'Platonism,' which is alien to the Bible. These theologians think they should do justice to the Bible by dismissing the idea of the continued life of the soul adhered to by Christianity for the past two thousand years.

Is this really what the Bible means? Should a Christianity orientated to the Bible really dispense with this universally Christian, truly 'ecumenical' idea that has prevailed till now? First of all we must add something on the approach to the topic. It cannot be expected that everything belonging to the realm of supersensible experience and knowledge must be comprehensively contained in the Bible if it is to be taken as true. Nowhere does the Bible lay claim to being *the* complete text book in relation to supersensible truths. It is not a compendium of metaphysics, but a document that testifies to a fact. It is the unique document of a divine activity that culminates in the deed of redemption of Golgotha. In testifying to this fact of salvation what concerned ideology was mentioned in passing if there was occasion for it. But the great comprehensive world picture, against the background of which the story of salvation occurs, is nowhere described as such. One could assume the elements of such a world picture, in which the supersensible had its place, to be still fairly general among men of those times. They still knew that there were angels, even several orders of angels, devils and evil spirits. They stood much closer to the supersensible realities. For example — when the priest Zechariah had had the vision of Gabriel and returned unable to speak from the Holy of Holies, the congregation praying outside was immediately aware that he must have had a supersensible experience during his service there (Luke 1:22). People knew that such things happened. One can certainly not say that of modern day people. If he is again to find a relationship to the biblical record, man must be helped to find an outlook in which the supersensible realities again have their place, as is the case with Rudolf Steiner's anthroposophy. This outlook cannot be built up from the Bible alone for the reasons given — that the Bible is not in this respect complete and does not intend to be. It is therefore not to be expected that everything concerning the supersensible must 'be in the Bible.' The survival of the soul could be a truth even if it were not expressly taught in the Bible.

However, that is certainly not the case. Reference to life after death does occur in the Bible. The theologians mentioned know that too, of course. They see themselves under the necessity of devaluing the implications of such passages and representing them as intrusions of 'heathen' doctrine that have penetrated no more than the fringes of the Bible. The really central message of the Bible, so they think, proffers the idea of the non-existence of the dead until the Last Day.

Let us see what the Bible has to say about that.

The *Old Testament,* it is true, is extraordinarily reticent about what concerns the continued existence of the soul. Where it rises prophetically to a hopeful outlook, it looks to the resurrection of the body at the end of days. Is there, then, no indication of anything between?

Not absolutely. There are several places that indicate an existence after death. When Abraham died, he was 'gathered to his people' (Gen.25:8). When this expression appears in connection with the other patriarchs, one could apply it to the burial chambers in Hebron where the bodies rest beside each other. But in Abraham's case it is different since his forefathers lay buried in Chaldea, in Ur and Haran. Therefore something supersensible is meant. Moreover, the Old Testament speaks occasionally of 'Sheol' as the abode of departed souls. It is a dark region, a shadowy world like the Greek 'Hades.'

Why is the view of life after death in the Old Testament so gloomy? The unique task of the people of Israel consisted in preparing the earthly body of the approaching Messiah. Thus there was a special way of looking at bodily existence on earth in Old Testament religion. The other side to this deeply justified interest was that bodiless existence could not be regarded and appreciated in the same degree. It was certainly known that the soul continued to exist after death, but this existence without the earthly body was felt to be an existence of a subordinate kind. In yet another but also similar way the *Greeks* came to their grey Hades. They were so full of the dignity and the beauty of the physical body that the loss of it was bound to weigh very heavily. 'Sheol' and 'Hades' were not just theories, but these pictures correspond to certain factual experiences of disembodied souls who, because of their high estimation of the earthly, did not find it easy after death to make themselves at home in the bodiless world.

Homer makes Achilles say he would rather be a beggar on earth than a king in the realm of shadows. Plato, who was also a Greek, could speak very differently thanks to the heritage of the ancient mystery schools where the soul became open to the supersensible through exercise and purification. Against the background of such special experience, Plato could glorify the grandeur of souls made free from the body, though he fell into the prejudice of undervaluing the significance of the earthly body by seeing it merely as a grave for the soul. He would not have cared for the Christian hope of a transfiguration of even the physical at the end of days. In his brushing aside the importance of the earthly body Plato was as one-sided as the Old Testament in its lack of interest in the disembodied soul.

Only in *Christianity* can the one-sided truths of the Old Testament and Platonism be harmoniously united in one picture of the true reality. Christianity concentrates on the resurrection of the body of Christ on Easter Day. It knows that for the Christian the attainment of such a resurrection body may be hoped for at the end of time, and that thereby man will for the first time be perfected in the God-likeness intended for him. But it is not therefore less aware of the continued life of the soul after death, even if in the New Testament this fact falls more into the background in face of the tremendous event of the resurrection of the body.

By the resurrection of his body Christ has already achieved what will only be accomplished for men on the Last Day. As the Savior died on Good Friday, the earth shook. On Easter Sunday it shook once more. Between these two dramatically accentuated moments, however, something happened in the silence that also belongs to the total event of Golgotha, and cannot be thought of apart from it. The fact that the dead body rested in the grave is not all there is to be said about the period between Death and Resurrection.

On Good Friday the crucified Christ spoke to the criminal: 'Truly, I say to you, today you will be with me in Paradise' (Luke 23:43). When someone is dying, a loosening and setting free of the soul may possibly already begin so that there are certain clairvoyant moments as it wrests itself from the body. Something like this must have been the case with the dying criminal. He must have perceived something about the one crucified with him, who outwardly looked nothing more than an unfortunate man in the last extremity, that enabled him to see in him the king of a heavenly realm. Christ is able to carry this soul that clings to him through the crisis of death — and in a few moments something of the greatest importance can happen in a man to change him — and allow him to share in his sunlit spiritual kingdom. As a result the criminal dies differently and goes towards a quite different kind of experience after death from what would otherwise have been the case. Here the Gospel speaks quite openly of an event that happens for the soul separated from the physical body. 'Today' does not refer to Easter Sunday. If one takes what Christ says as it stands, it can mean only the situation directly after death.

This opens for us the door to that mysterious happening that Christian tradition has called the descent to those in the underworld *(descensus ad infernos)* or, not altogether correctly, the descent into hell — the 'harrowing of hell.' It is not a question of 'hell' but of 'Sheol' or 'Hades.' '... I have the keys of Death and Hades' says the Risen One in the Revelation of John (1:19). This journey to Hades is clearly mentioned in the First Letter of Peter (3:19; 4:6) and we hear of it in the Letter to the Ephesians (4:9). It is a basic part of the original Christian belief, and was taken up as a separate article in the Apostles' Creed. Christ was not swallowed up by death in the time till Easter Day, but had a real and fully conscious existence as an excarnated soul.

Modern theology regards this biblical statement as the typical mythological way of speaking 'conditioned by the times.' This is correct insofar as the idea of a kingdom of the dead to be found 'under the earth' has no place in today's scientific world picture. Within this purely materialistic world picture the ancient view of the three-tier Heaven, Earth, Underworld is obviously impossible. But if one speaks of the ancient world picture being 'conditioned by the times,' it is not good enough simply then to reject that world picture. One should see that for men of old the purely material experience of the world was still permeated in many ways by experiences of a supersensible kind; the two were interwoven. Today we can neatly divide them. The 'three tiers' are connected with what was seen by unsophisticated men as an Above and a Below. However there went along with this picture an experience of supersensible reality that was 'set in motion' by the related sense impressions. The impression made by the picture of the visible 'heaven' disposed the soul to be touched by a 'higher' world beyond the spatial. The Hades-underworld is the pictorial expression for a supersensible realm that again as such is beyond spatiality, where disembodied souls live as it were 'in the shadow' cast by their lives on earth. In the experience of the departed soul this earthly life, with all its culpability and estrangement from its divine source, thrusts itself in front of the spiritual sun. The soul finds itself 'in the shadow of the earth.' Thus Hades can be understood as a 'soul-landscape,' as a 'soul-place.' The disembodied Christ-soul entered this world and became as we say in the Creed of The Christian Community 'the helper of the souls of the dead who had lost their divine nature.' Christ was able to do this because in his holy life on earth he had not lost the divine nature, and, as a result, in death his soul could immediately enter that 'Paradise' which clearly as little means something spatial-geographical as the 'underworld' or the 'prison' of which Peter's letter speaks.

The truth of the further life of the soul after death is centrally anchored in the New Testament by Christ's descent into Hades.

One should also think of the Transfiguration, in the course of which Moses and Elijah — that is, souls living in the other world — appear in glory and converse with the transfigured Christ about his approaching death (Luke 9:30f). Moses and Elijah are therefore by no means 'dead.' They look with great concern at what happens on earth.

Christ taught 'as one having authority, and not as the scribes.' That is also valid for the words with which he spoke of the life of the soul after death. These occur first and foremost in the story of 'the rich man and poor Lazarus' (Luke 16:19-31). It is not exactly a 'parable,' nor is it called one by the Gospel, but tells a story from life. One could speak of a 'parable' only insofar as the fire in which the rich gourmand suffers his torment is no physical fire but an absolutely appropriate picture of the truth, just like 'Abraham's bosom.' The story allows us to see quite clearly how souls have a consciousness after death that extends not only to their own destiny but also to other souls, even indeed those remaining behind in earthly existence. Christ told this story since he had insight into the world beyond. If similar ideas are shown to exist in the Judaism of those times, then Christ has confirmed them as correct by his own words. He also points at times in other contexts to the further life of the soul after death. A man should practise conciliation whilst he is still 'on the way' with

89

another lest he come to prison, which he cannot leave before
he has paid the last farthing (Matt.5:25f). One should not be
afraid of those who can kill only the body but not the soul
(Matt.10:28). The dispute with the Sadducees — 'he is not
God of the dead, but of the living' — is primarily about
resurrection, but if Christ says that Abraham, Isaac and Jacob
as living souls already now belong to God, not only at the Last
Day, then that also indicates that we are not annihilated when
we die, '... for all live to him' (Luke 20:38).

The New Testament also speaks of how Christ and the power
of his redemptive deed should then be taken up by *individual
Christians*. Such solidarity with Christ — 'Christ in me, I in
Christ' — bears within it the certainty of overcoming death.
And not only in relation to the Last Day. 'He who believes in
the Son *has* eternal life' (John 3:36). He *has* it already now,
even if not in the absolutely final fullness of the Last Day
when 'the last enemy,' the death of the body, will also be
rendered powerless. This is just what John's Gospel says (5:24;
6:54). This 'already now' by no means precludes the fulfilment
of the Last Day (6:39f,44,54). As far as the soul is concerned,
however, death is beaten from the field even *before* the Last
Day: '... if any one keeps my word, he will never see death'
(8:51). The Christ-permeated man will still have to die bodily,
but for him death goes no further: 'he who believes in me,
though he die, yet shall he live' (11:25).

The first death of a Christian recorded by the New Testament, the death of Stephen, certainly does not call up the
impression of a soul preparing to enter 'the long night of
death' until the Last Day. On the contrary it is an absolutely
triumphant crossing into the higher world opening before him.
'I see the heavens opened, and the Son of Man standing at the
right hand of God' (Acts 7:56). Therefore when the expression
'fall asleep' is used for death (7:60), we should consider that
the point of comparison does not necessarily lie in the fact that
we more or less lose consciousness on falling asleep. It can

just as well be seen in the fact that when we fall asleep, there is the slipping out of the soul from its physical body that also happens, though more profoundly, at death. Stephen 'fell asleep' — his soul left his body. Nothing is said there about the kind of consciousness of the excarnated soul, only about the process of leaving the body.

The original Christians certainly did not experience their dead martyrs as unconscious sleepers in the beyond, though these like Stephen were 'fallen asleep.' That they were living and active in the spirit was a fundamental experience. The Letter to the Hebrews speaks of the 'spirits of just men made perfect' (12:23). From the early Christian experience of the helping nearness of the world of the dead springs the wonderfully comforting picture of being 'surrounded by so great a cloud of witnesses' (Heb.12:1). Nor are the martyrs by any means sleeping spirits according to the Revelation of John; they are conscious and active. Twice the 'souls' *(psychai)* are specifically mentioned (6:9; 20:4); they have therefore separated their existence from the body before the Last Day. The 'first resurrection' in which these souls participate is an anticipation of the awakening in the spirit which will be completed only at the end of days in the resurrection that includes the body.

In harmony with this there also stand the direct statements of great Christian personalities in the New Testament who, out of their Christian feeling for life, look towards their approaching death. In the Second Letter of Peter we find the expression: 'as long as I am in this body [tent]' (2Pet.1:13). There is no mention of that indivisible unity of body and soul postulated by modern theology in the wake of materialism. The nearer the soul comes to death and the closer it is united with Christ, the more it feels itself as something independent of the body. The body becomes a 'tent' that the soul leaves behind in death. The passage continues: 'I know that the putting off of my body (tent) will be soon, as our Lord Jesus Christ showed me' (1:14). It is therefore a supersensible knowledge that he has about his imminent death. 'The putting off' of the 'tent' is indicated in what follows by the word *exodos,* Latin *exitus,* 'departure' (1:15). Still today the expression 'exitus' is used for death in medical terminology. One would wish that those who speak of 'exitus' in this sense would take the expression quite literally. It clearly does not say that death is the end but that a 'departure' occurs. Is it then ancient superstition or 'Platonism' that intrudes as something alien in the New Testament with these expressions about 'putting off the tent' and 'departing'? Is it not much rather in harmony with the sacred experiences of so many dying Christians throughout two thousand years?

In a similar way Paul faces his approaching death. He feels it already near, but is inwardly torn in two. On the one hand it requires him to 'dissolve' *(analysai)* his union with the body 'and be with Christ' (Phil.1:23). On the other hand his sense of duty urges him to persevere in his body with the communities entrusted to him. Here it is obvious that he is not thinking of the Last Day, but that he expects this being 'with Christ' immediately after death. Thus for him the revaluation of values can take place. Dying — which for men bound to the material is the essence of 'loss' since it means losing all with the earthly body — turns for Paul into a 'gain.' 'For to me to live is Christ, and to die is gain' (1:21).

Such testimonies of an indestructible awareness of victory over death seem to us to proceed truly from the very centre of a living experience of Christ.

That the hope of resurrection on the Last Day suffers no injury by a continued life of the soul after death we hope we have sufficiently stressed. One does not exclude the other. On the contrary. The true foundation for the hope of a final transformation of even the body actually lies in the fact that the light of immortality already shines forth from the soul united with Christ.

14. The Ascension of Christ

Luke told the story of Christ's Ascension twice: at the end of his Gospel and at the beginning of his Acts of the Apostles. The One, The Unique One and the Lonely One stands at the centre in the twenty-four chapters of his Gospel. He dies and transforms himself into the Risen One. He experiences a further transformation through the Ascension: He grows into the widths of space and cosmic greatness. He again wins the divine heavenly dimensions for human nature, which he had taken into himself and transfigured. He achieves that limitless mode of being by virtue of which he can encompass and span the whole of humanity and all the earth. That which emerges in this way as the crowning end of the Gospel, at the same time forms the presupposition of the Acts of the Apostles, which now gives an account of the many who became Christians.

As Luke begins his Acts of the Apostles, he first looks back at his Gospel as the 'first book' that he has 'made.' There, he has taken the narrative 'until the day when [Christ] was taken up.' He further added the important supplement that the appearance of the Risen One lasted forty days. Next, he immediately draws the reader into the situation of the last discourse, which the Risen One had held with his people on the Mount of Olives. The last words run: 'and you shall be my witnesses in Jerusalem and in all Judea and Samaria and to the ends of the earth' (Acts 1:8). The growth into the widths of space lies in this sequence: Jerusalem, Judea, Samaria, the ends of the earth.

In Jerusalem, Christ went through the most terrible contraction of his heavenly-derived being in the experience of earthly, human death. 'I have a baptism to be baptized with; and how I am constrained until it is accomplished' (Luke 12:50). With these words, he has expressed his feeling for life at the approach of death. 'How I am constrained' — literally: 'How I am pressed together.' The new spreading and becoming expansive started with the Resurrection and Ascension and became 'omnipresence' over the whole earth. This process of spreading out first makes the diffusion of Christianity comprehensible. 'Christianity does not expand through the world in the footsteps of the Apostles, but Christians follow the footsteps of the Lord with their missionary activity.'*

It is not what is today called propaganda, in which you make other people believe something which would otherwise have been quite alien to them. The wandering Apostles were in truth 'drawn along' by the Christ being, which poured itself out into the widths of space. Basically, on earth they only try to follow after his ubiquity, which is founded on the Ascension. Basically, they only try to make people everywhere conscious of a reality, which came into being through Christ's deed, and of which each man must have knowledge if he wishes to become a true human being. Something of this reality lives in the divining depths of the soul; otherwise the mission would not meet with the strength of 'faith.'

From Jerusalem to the 'ends of the earth.' 'Earth' is the last word of the disappearing Risen One. His gaze and his will are directed to the whole earth. The saying of Archimedes has been transmitted: 'Give me the appropriate standpoint in space, and from there I will unhinge the whole earth.' He referred to the law of the lever, which dawned on him. To be able to lift the earth with all its weight, he would need a point of application outside the earth. In a similar way, Christ, through his elevation to heavenly being, had to find the point of application from which he was able to get near to transfiguring and transforming the earthly. He is, to speak in the language of our ritual, raised to heavenly being *for* earthly being.

After Christ had spoken his last words about the 'ends of the earth,' the actual Ascension-Event starts. 'As they were

* Kurt von Wistinghausen, *Das neue Bekenninis,* p. 69.

looking on, he was lifted up' (Acts 1:9). It is not a question of a process within crass material substance, which would have been visible to everyone, but a question of something which took place before the opened souls of the disciples.

The narrative of the Acts of the Apostles is significantly supplemented here through an otherwise scanty account, which Luke has given at the close of his Gospel, that the Risen One 'lifting up his hands ... blessed them' (Luke 24:50) at his Ascension. So this Ascension is not like the departure of someone who takes his leave and turns round to start on his journey, at the same time turning his back on those staying behind. Christ remains fully turned towards his people. Indeed, he is turned towards them as fully as he can be: he spreads his arms over them, he blesses them — that means, he lets his being stream towards them, he is there wholly for them. But does it say 'he parted from them'? (Luke 24:51). The Greek word is from the same stem as the word 'distance.' A distance grew between the blessing Christ and the disciples, an increasing, intermediate space. The blessing empathy towards them does not stop, but doubtless the process of perception by the disciples does stop.

The Risen One transfigures himself to a still more elevated, to a still more spiritualized mode of being. In relation to this, the disciples' power of perception comes to its limit. They no longer keep up, their consciousness does not keep step with the tremendous thing that is happening here. He 'outgrows' their supersensory power of perception. and just this is represented in the image — the way the One raising himself disappears from their view.

This process of being 'carried up,' of which the end of Luke's Gospel speaks, has its parallel in the process of being 'lifted up' in the account of the Acts of the Apostles, to which we will now turn. The Greek word for 'lifted' contains a reference to the element of air. So we can say one 'airs' something through lifting it up. The powers of 'lightness' act in relation to weight as they hold sway in air and light.

Our earthly expressions never measure up to supersensory events. Each word image always contains a one-sidedness, just as each appropriate simile is always lame somewhere. Therefore, to arrive approximately at the process which is meant, we must bring the various expressions used together. He was 'carried up' (Luke 24:51), and he was 'lifted up' (Acts 1:9). The first time the carrying forces of the Father are experienced, the second time more the powers of lightness and of the light which lift the Risen One up into still higher glory.

Yet a third word is used: Christ was 'taken up' (Acts 1:2,11). Heaven 'takes' him up. It is something like taking communion of the highest kind. Human nature which Christ had taken upon himself and transformed through his death and Resurrection, is received by the higher worlds. Humanity, consecrated through Christ, is a new enriching element for the heavens, and is not only spiritualized and ensouled, but also 'embodied.' In this sense, noted earlier in his Gospel, Luke summarized the whole Mystery of Golgotha, from death through Resurrection till Ascension in the words 'taking up.' 'When the days drew near for him to be received up, [taken up], he set his face to go to Jerusalem' (Luke 9:51).

In these three cases, it is expressed passively. He is carried, he is lifted, he is taken (or received). Something happens to him. This can also be said actively. The Risen One 'went' into heaven (Acts 1:10). In the original text, we read the same word that is used for the going of Jesus from Galilee up to Jerusalem, and similarly for when the Risen One walked with the two disciples to Emmaus. The meaning indicated by earthly 'going,' to be in active movement towards a goal, takes its continuation also in the supersensible. In the realm of souls and spirits, too, ways are walked. So Ascension is both something which happens to Christ, as well as something which is his very own doing. The truth meant here lies at the point where these two (on an earthly plane, contradictory) assertions coincide.

Similarly, a contradiction exists between the two descriptions: the receding, blessing figure, and the One 'going into Heaven.' One aspect of the event is taken up in each of these descriptions. Both pictures, each in itself bringing an experience to expression, together yield an impression of what happened at that time.

The further 'going' of the Raised One was veiled by a cloud. The form is lost to the disciples' view. However, the supersensible experience has not yet come to an end with all this. They have not fallen back into everyday consciousness. 'And while they were gazing into heaven as he went, behold, two men stood by them in white robes' (Acts 1:10). Just as at the empty grave early on Easter morning, so here, two angels appear beside the emptied field of vision. The disciples do not only see them, they can also apprehend the angels' words in their spiritual hearing. Just as the angels at the tomb ask Mary Magdalene why she was weeping, so here a question stands at the beginning 'Men of Galilee, why do you stand looking into heaven?' (Acts 1:11).

It could appear as if such questions, directed from higher beings to earthly men, were meant 'educationally' from the superiority of the wiser. This might well play a part under certain circumstances. But couldn't these questions be genuine and seriously meant? Beings meet who belong to quite different worlds. No wonder that the earthly partner usually has to overcome a deep fright, if the 'completely different' confronts him. But couldn't it happen the other way round, that the materially bound man evokes deep consternation in the other world? On Easter morning, jubilation held sway in the realm of the angels.

How strange it must appear to the angels that a human soul yields to his desperate grief, a human soul which, since the Easter event, had only perceived the negative picture of the empty tomb. So at Ascension might the angels also be surprised about the strange mortals, who stare painfully at that place where only a moment ago there was something, and where there is now nothing more for their failing spiritual gaze. The Greek word which is rendered in English as 'gaze' signifies a seeing with an intention, with a willing-seeing, which would like to apprehend something definite visually. But this exerted looking now goes into the void, its object has withdrawn from it. The angels must perhaps first get used to the soul-disposition of these mortals and to become aware as to what possibilities they do or do not have in this higher kind of seeing. But then they can bestow on them their angelic comfort. 'This Jesus, who was taken up from you into heaven, will come in the same way as you saw him go into heaven' (Acts 1:11).

With that, the bridge to the future is forged. The gaze falls prophetically on the return of Christ which, according to the promise of the Gospel, will become apparent 'on the clouds of heaven.' On the same Mount of Olives on which the Ascension was experienced, Christ spoke on the Tuesday of Holy Week of this return. The sphere of the clouds is that part of the earthly realm where the earth, in its atmospheric and in its fine etheric material forms of water and air, stands open to heaven's interweaving. From the clouds of heaven, which in their continual lively forming and transforming activity animate and arouse the soul's power of observation, Christ will show himself anew to human beings when he 'comes,' when he makes a movement of his own accord towards the consciousness of human beings.

In the rendering of this angel promise, Luke introduces another word to do with vision: Christ will return in the same way as they saw him go into the heavenly worlds. Here is a new, solemn kind of seeing. When the hour of return is here, the gap which has arisen in the consciousness of mankind will close.

The new vision will again join on to where it was broken off at that time on the fortieth day after Easter, when the Risen One outgrew his people's faculty of perception.

15. Walking with the Risen One
— the way to Emmaus

Luke's narrative about the way to Emmaus speaks directly to the heart. It places the content of archetypal human experience before our souls: the shared way of those bearing sorrow, the conversation on the way, entering the house, the meal. But the most profound mystery of our earth existence accompanies and plays into these ordinary events of human life: the resurrection.

The 'resurrection on the Last Day' is the long-range objective presaged from afar for the earthly human being. But it has its everyday image each morning when we straighten up from lying down and 'get up.' We do this with thoughtless matter-of-factness, until perhaps sometimes an illness provides us with a little consciousness of what it means to be able to get up. As often as we raise ourselves into the vertical we carry out in brief what we had to learn with great effort as children. The upright stance is a manifestation of the truly human, as is our walking on two feet a consequence of it. Walking is not only a biological function serving, as with the animal, essential locomotion. We would not apply the phrase 'way of life' to the existence of an animal. Human movement in walking takes into itself something higher. We speak of the 'way of life' whereby 'wayfaring' is open both to 'going on the way' and to 'changing our way.' The Old Testament speaks mysteriously of Enoch who lived in grey antiquity: 'he walked with God' and was taken up into the invisible (Gen.5:4).

Human movement is wonderfully composed into the rhythm of the cosmos. If a wanderer could pace forwards uninterruptedly in a leisurely reflective tempo he would come round the earth in 365 days, corresponding to the sun year. Is it a coincidence that this same number of the sun year appears in connection with Enoch who walks with God in that the age of 365 years is ascribed to him?

On Easter morning Christ, anticipating the Last Day, rested his earthly human body from the powers of death and let it resurrect. As the Resurrected One he is now involved in an advancing movement of a higher kind, because also in the realm of spirits there is 'progress,' 'advance.' In the Apocalypse Christ promises his disciples in Sardis that they will 'walk with him.'

The Risen One walks spiritually with the two disciples who are walking on their way to Emmaus on Easter afternoon. Together they search for the meaning of what they have just experienced as something incomprehensible which weighs heavily on their souls. That walking together can be conducive to a common searching for the truth is a well-known phenomenon. Plato lets his conversationalists in his late work *The Laws* develop their thoughts on a walk which takes them from Knossos to a temple of Zeus. The peripatetic school of philosophy takes its name from 'moving along,' *peripatein.* (This word also occurs in the Emmaus Story, 24:17.) Through the seriousness of their common striving after knowledge *(syn-zētein,* 'to look for in common') the two Emmaus disciples create the precondition for the Risen One, stepping forward unnoticed out of the Easter landscape towards evening, to associate himself with them and to bring his step into harmony with their walking pace. 'He approached them.' The two are so absorbed in their conversation that the approach and addition of the Third is hardly noticed. So he walks with them, listening, silent.

This silent accompanying must have lasted a considerable time. (The Greek uses the imperfect here, 24:15, to express what is lasting.) But then he breaks the spell of his silence. He speaks.

And in so doing he opens up a second realm of the truly human in addition to walking upright. All attempts to derive the speaking of man from the sound-utterances of the animal only reveal a blindness to the spiritual impact from above with which we are concerned in the human word. This cannot be understood from below. It has descended from higher worlds 'which are penetrated by the pure living way of God's word' as Goethe said in his *West-Eastern Divan.* Christ is indeed himself God's word, the Logos. And as he now entered into the rhythm of the disciples' walking, so he now also weaves his speaking into theirs.

His speaking is first of all a questioning. 'What kind of words are these which you are exchanging with one another as you walk?' Why does Christ ask? Has he then not noticed that they are really talking the whole time of nothing else but the events of the past days, but of him? They cannot for their part comprehend his questions so they respond with another question. 'Are you the only one in Jerusalem who does not know about these events?' And again a question comes, 'Which events?'

How are we to understand this questioning? Is it only meant pedagogically rather like a teacher eliciting a piece of knowledge from a pupil which he himself already knows? Or are we to think of a quite original 'genuine' questioning? Could it be that the Risen One, coming from experiences which lie completely outside the consciousness of the disciples, had to bridge over something like an abyss of a growing alienation? Did he not first have to live again into the soul condition of those who during his passage through death, despite the shock to their souls, nevertheless continued their former existence? From their words he was confronted by how his destiny appeared from outside. Perhaps it was significant for him to have this view brought to him from earthly human beings. So he listens to what his own followers say about Jesus of Nazareth.

They express what he meant to them in a kind of declaration of faith: 'Jesus of Nazareth ... a prophetic man, mighty in deed and word ... they condemned and crucified him ... we had hoped he would save Israel.' This avowal goes so far as to recognize the great prophet but it stops short exactly where the actual mystery starts. The grave may have been empty on this morning, the women may have seen something, but of the disciples who then went to the grave it is only said (mirroring the resignation of 'we had hoped'): 'They did not see him.' Here their Christology ends. The light shining from the prophetic figure is extinguished with the death on the cross and leaves them in an even deeper darkness.

Christ sees that he must give them some support in their consciousness. He takes a third step towards them. He enters into their thinking which is so very much in need of illumination.

Modern science wrestles more keenly than ever with the problem of the origin of the human being. In this three basic questions are constantly raised. How did man come to his upright gait? How did he learn to speak? How did he develop into a thinking being? One tries in vain to understand all this in terms of an evolution out of the animal world. Rudolf Steiner demonstrated a long time ago a quite different way to the solution of these three problems. He often showed from his spiritual vision how these three faculties, which only develop after birth, are brought into being in the first years of the child with the help of the highest spiritual powers.

We might have expected just our technical age to be able to see these faculties which earlier ages had taken for granted in quite a new light. At a time when our means of transport are so overdeveloped we could rediscover the miracle of our own ability to walk. In the age of radio and tape we could feel all the more deeply the mystery that lives in the directly spoken word. In the age of the electronic brain a new possibility opens up to grasp how it differs from truly creative thinking.

Gait — word — thought, this triad also determines the sequence of the Emmaus story.

Taking the picture into consideration which the disciples had gained of him and of his destiny, Christ now uses human thought forms in order to try and get his divine knowledge across to them. This cannot be done without a feeling of divine pain, 'O foolish men, and slow of heart.' For a being of a higher order which can comprehend the most diverse span of factors in split-second intuitions, the brain-bound thinking of earthly beings must appear obtuse and sluggish and it must be painful to have to adapt to this kind of thinking. 'Foolish men'; in the original text *a-nóētoi,* those standing outside *nous,* the perceptive spirit reason. 'And slow of heart,' earthly man has certainly become adept in the use of his intellect, but the heart organ, without whose participation knowledge of a higher kind is not possible, has lost much of its sensitivity and become 'sluggish.'

But Christ did not stop at this painful feeling of alienation. He sought in love, despite the inability of men to understand, to prepare the way for his great mystery to enter the thought world of earthly man. Since both disciples are pious Jews he links on to what already lies prepared in their souls about Moses and the prophets. He lets the pictures, which had become awesome and dark with age, become transparent, as when the sun's rays lighten up the colourful windows of a cathedral. Luke here uses the word *dihermēneuein* in which is contained the name of the messenger of the god Hermes (Mercury), who is the genius of all mediation. Shedding light in this way on the Old Testament leads them to an ever greater grasp of the fact which provides the entry into the whole of his teaching: 'Must not Christ suffer all this to enter into his glory?'

It is the truth of suffering which is expressed here, albeit in another form to the one preached half a millenium earlier by Buddha. All earthly human existence, so Buddha had taught, is unavoidably pervaded by suffering. This suffering is for him in itself a valid objection to human existence. If we want to be liberated from pain, our will to live must be completely eradicated. Then all earthly incarnation and existence will come to an end. According to this view the whole development up till now of the personality in an earthly body appears as a wrong path of evolution which has to be put right. Thus Buddha. Rudolf Steiner has described how Christ corrected Buddhism, not theoretically or doctrinally but 'practically,' since through his act of salvation he created an altered world situation within which the consequence of negation need not be drawn any more. New possibilities appear: out of all the bad all the greater good can come into being. In the light of the change brought about through the deed of Christ suffering can appear in a totally new context. For only through taking suffering upon himself could Christ attain to that revelation of glory through which also the stigmata are transfigured.

For Buddha, his deep insights were not the abstract opinion of a scholar but the result of a path, an inner way, which he had gone. His teaching was gained in 'walking the way.' The teaching on suffering which the Risen One gives to the disciples is a truth 'on the way' in a still higher sense. Luke's account is significant even in its apparently unimportant details. We see how after Christ's first question the disciples stop walking. Surprised and sadly bewildered they 'stood still' (24:17). But then, reading between the lines, we gather that his words of teaching brought them into movement again, for 'they drew near to the village to which they were going' (24:28).

The way leads to the goal. Both disciples see the house before them which is to receive them. But does not Christ seem to wish to walk further? (24:28). It is not a matter of course that their being in company with Christ should continue into the house. The disciples have come into contact with a being of the higher world on their way. This contact has its own momentum. If it is to continue into the quite different setting of the house the disciples have to do something out of their own initiative to retain the presence of the Lord with them. They have to 'invite' him.

In the house the experience of the disciples finds its last enhancement and also its end. The Risen One sits with them at table. He holds the meal with them, linking on to the meals which he had celebrated with his own until the Last Supper on Maundy Thursday. It is absolutely a matter of course for the evangelist to give his account here in just that ritual stylization which we know from the great feedings and from the Last Supper, that he spoke the blessing, that he 'took' bread and 'broke' it and 'gave' it to his own. The one who offers the meal is not only teacher, he is also dispenser of substance. He himself is the bread of life which is experienced in the communion as a creative, constructive force right into the bodily nature. In this act the bodily nature is affirmed.

Buddha strove to eliminate the deeply rooted will to live and to make the reconstruction of the earthly body impossible in order to effect a final escape from suffering. This goal of his is represented by him in a highly suggestive metaphor: 'House-builder [the power which builds up the house of the body], you are discovered! Never again will you build the home. Your beams are broken up and the roof of your house falled in.'* This metaphor is directed against the carpenter whose work is to come to nothing. But Jesus was a carpenter! His profession was the building of the house with beams and ridge. Christ speaks of it when he said he would 'build up in three days' the demolished Temple, the 'temple of his body' (John 2:21). What Buddha negates is here divinely affirmed. Christ built the resurrection body as his eternal 'home.' Through the communion he now wishes to build the eternal home of a resurrection body for human beings, which is to be completed on the Last Day. Then they may be permitted to live in this body, fashioned out of immortality — when the day of outer world existence will have declined and evening will have descended on all outer life.

---

* Compare Rudolf Frieling. *Christianity and Reincarnation,* p.59.

16. The power of transformation: Insights of St Paul

Paul's life and work follow the motif of transformation. The persecutor of Christ becomes a disciple of Christ, Saul becomes Paul. It is out of this background of destiny that the words should be read which Paul wrote in his letters on the theme of transformation; not as 'armchair-theology,' but as something which has been concrete experience. It is as if he tries to narrow down what is difficult to express by making use of different words which the Greek language has placed at his disposal. In what follows, three such different statements will be considered alongside one another.

1. Transformation

In order to make clear the difference between the Old and the New Covenant, Paul refers (2Cor.3) to the Old Testament story of the shining face of Moses (Exod.34:29-35). For forty days and forty nights Moses had remained in the holy sphere of Mount Sinai and the Lord had spoken to him *face to face, as a man speaks to his friend* (Exod.33:11). Through this, Moses' face had become radiant as a reflection of this divine 'confrontation.' The Israelites were not strong enough to bear this other-worldly radiance when Moses returned to them, and so he covered his shining face with a veil.

As a further development of this motif, Paul sees as in a picture how a humanity which has not yet been touched by Christ also wears a veil before its face. This restriction of vision stems from the heart which, too, is covered by a veil. If a man finds Christ, then this veil is removed. In becoming a Christian he receives 'enlightenment,' because Christ works together with the Holy Spirit who brings insight and understanding. *The Lord is the Spirit* (2Cor.3:17). The view is cleared for seeing the divine. In the fourth chapter of the Second Letter to the Corinthians, Paul describes the process with the words:

The God who said, 'Let light shine out of darkness,'
has given a bright light in our hearts for the
enlightenment *[phōtismos]* of knowledge *[gnōsis]* of
the revealing glory *[doxa]* of God in the face of Jesus
Christ (4:6).

For Paul, this process is of equal rank with *Let there be light* on the first day of creation.

In this connection Paul formulates the sentence about the transformation of a Christian which concerns us here:

We all, with unveiled faces reflecting the revealing
glory of the Lord, are being transformed into the same
likenesses from clarity to clarity as from the Lord of
the Spirit (2Cor.3:18).

This concentrated saying is heavily laden with meaning. It is necessary to take the time to consider it word for word. The sentence begins exultantly with the Whitsun-like 'we all.' What was reserved for Moses alone in the Old Testament shall now become possible for all Christians. The original text does not say 'is reflected in us' but *we* reflect, it is our activity. The picture of a mirror is not meant in a negative sense here, glassy cold, distorting and indistinct; it is meant positively, as when a stormy and wildly lashing sea comes to rest and the heavenly stars can be seen in its smooth surface. We reflect the glory of the Lord when our active inner effort stills the storms of the soul, and we hold up this calm sea to the divine revelation in devoted expectation.

In so doing we 'expose' ourselves to the divine image and give it the opportunity to create in us. In the kingdoms of nature the divine images work by a kind of compulsion. The rose is not asked whether it wants to become a rose; it is shaped and developed by its archetypal image as a matter of course. With human begins it is different. We can hide from the radiance of our archetypal divine image, or on the other hand expose ourselves in freedom to this radiance. *Where the Spirit of the Lord is, there is freedom* (2Cor.3:17). Through brightness of heart, we can devote our beholding with unveiled face to Christ, who is the archetypal image above all others. As the Son born in eternity he is the likeness of the Father. *He is the image of the invisible God* (Col.1:15). According to the intention of the divine Creator, man is to become the likeness of God (Gen.1:26).

A likeness makes like: whoever devotes his soul to the influence of a picture receives a transforming influence which, in an imperceptible, intimate way, makes him like to the picture. 'We become changed into the same likeness.' For 'changing,' Paul here uses *metamorphoein,* 'transform.'

Such a transformation can only happen quite gradually. It is a matter of a process, a development by degrees: 'from one clarity to another.' In this way, a delicate soul-process is indicated which is not dependent on whether an authentic portrait has been preserved for us from the turning-point of time, which, of course, it has not. But it is intimate experience that for him who takes the content of the Gospels into his heart, a countenance, at first maybe more or less dark, then gradually growing clearer, can begin to appear; a face which is unmistakably 'known' to a Christian.

2. Reshaping

Paul approaches the mystery of transformation from another side in his letter to the Philippians:

Our home is in the heavens
from whence we also await the Saviour
the Lord Jesus Christ

who will re-shape our lowly body
so that it will be of equal form with the body of glory
according to the power of working
by which he is able to subject all things to himself.
(Phil.3:20f).

This time, it is primarily Christ who acts. We await his return from the heavenly worlds where we ourselves originally were at home. The word for 'transformation' this time is *metaschēmatizein,* re-schematize. Here it important to find the right understanding of the word 'scheme.' It has already been used by Paul in this same letter to the Philippians, before the passage we are now considering, and actually referring to Christ himself. 'He emptied himself and took on the form and appearance of a servant, entering into the likeness of Man, and was found in his *schēma* as a human being' (Phil.2:7). The Latin translation here renders *schēma* as *habitus (habitu inventus ut homo), habitus,* as it were, 'having had.' In French and English the words habit, habitation and habitude are derived from *habitus.* What a man is comes to expression in his habits which he in-habits. *Schēma* as *habitus,* then, is something like an arrangement of life-patterns which is repeated. It is only when actual life goes out of the life-patterns, so that a mere empty, automatic mechanism is left, that the words scheme and schematic acquire unfortunate overtones. Here in the New Testament, however, the word *schēma* is meant positively, full of vitality. Inhabiting rhythms of 'going out' and 'going in' means reaching to the rhythms of exhaling and inhaling of the breath and rhythms of the pulsating blood. Christ works into this realm of life and penetrates it with a life of heavenly rhythm.

The world of rhythmically ordered life has always been the sphere of religious practice, and that is also true of Christianity. In the very concept of religious practice, the element of repetitive 'again and again' is inherent; hallowing of morning and evening, regular prayer, the holy year with its continuous sacramental worship. All this is for the service of Christ, who lets the liberations of a higher, heavenly life work into the coarse vibrations of our earth-bound bodily nature, right into pulse and breath.

3. Making completely anew

In the fifteenth chapter of the First Letter to the Corinthians it is the theme of resurrection which leads the apostle to the question of transformation. Here he does not speak of altering or re-shaping. Here Paul uses the word *allassein,* 'make different.' *Allassein* is a word of immediate elementary experience, not as thought-based as alteration and reshaping. With surprise and wonder the experience of 'different' is felt, with a nuance of 'quite different.'

This time the point of departure is the possibility of transformation of substance as such. Paul draws attention to the different qualities of the flesh, *sarx,* in the bodily natures of man and animal.

Not all flesh *[sarx]* is the same flesh,
for that of man is different,
that of the animals is different,
that of the birds is different,
that of the fishes is different (1Cor.15:39).

This continues upwards into the different qualities of the heavenly bodies, where, instead of 'flesh,' the *doxa* appears. The heavenly bodies show 'flesh,' the *doxa* appears. The heavenly bodies show differences in the aura-like light-qualities of their radiance.

There is a different light-quality to the radiance
of the sun,
a different one of the moon,
a different one of the stars,
and each different star differs from every other star
through its different light-quality (1Cor.15:41)

In between there is man. Like the animals, he bears a

perishable earthly body. Eventually, he is to become a bearer of a starry imperishable body of light. This transition is only possible through death and the power of resurrection:

See, I tell you a mystery. We shall not all fall asleep, but we shall all be transformed into something quite different, in the atom, in the twinkling of the eye at the last trumpet. For the trumpet will sound, and the dead will be awakened imperishable. and we shall be transformed into what is quite different. (1Cor.15:51f).

The conception of the atom as that which is finally indivisible leads to the limits of the spatial and opens the gaze beyond it to the 'super-spatial' which is 'quite different.' Similarly, the momentary blinking of the eye leads to the limits of measured time and gives a glimpse of the 'super-temporal' which, again, is 'quite different.' Through this total transformation, death, as the last enemy, is overcome. He is 'swallowed up in victory' (15:54). 'Swallowed up,' in the Greek: 'drunk down' *(katapinein),* as when a baby takes a drink into itself and so disposes of it, comes to terms with it. In Latin: *absorpta est mors,* 'absorbed.' The same word can be found in the Second Letter to the Corinthians (5:4), where the reference is to what is mortal being swallowed up by life. This nuance of absorption is of great importance. The experience of death is not simply pushed aside. It is to be worked through inwardly, thereby to deepen and augment the higher life even more, just because of having been absorbed.

When we place the three sayings about transformation from three different letters of Paul into this sequence, then they harmonize as a triad. In the sentence about reflecting and being transformed there breathes the air of freedom of the Holy . Spirit, with and through whom Christ works. The sentence about re-shaping in the letter to the Philippians speaks particularly about the living and working of the returning Christ. In the resurrection-chapter of the First Letter to the Corinthians, the contemplation descends right into the depths of the alchemy of substance. It is here that Paul uses the word 'mystery' (15:51). Material substance is the real world-riddle not the spirit. The spirit 'explains itself.' Matter remains dark, as long as it is not made plain, 'explained' and ultimately transfigured by the spirit. In matter the spirit goes beyond itself, 'ex-pressing' and emptying itself. In this chapter, Paul looks towards a distant fulfilment of the world, when the Son shall return a transformed creation to the Father. This saying about transformation, which we have dealt with here in third place, shows the working of Christ in its connection with the mystery of the Father.

The Transfiguration

17. Preliminaries

In theological circles today it is taken as self-evident truth that the wondrous stories found in the gospels belong to the realm of the mythical or legendary and thereby stand outside reality. For a long time now theology has accepted the perception of the world currently held by the natural sciences, as if there were no alternative at all.

Does it have to remain like this? So much is clear in any case that, within the framework of the only world-view scientifically accepted today, the gospels can only fall victim to corruption and disintegration. All the intelligence brought to bear on them can only destroy them. There is, however, the possibility of this intelligence advancing with insight to the point where it becomes conscious of its own limitations in relation to world-reality, where it becomes aware of its own relativity, where it perceives that an essential part of reality simply slips through the much too wide-meshed net it has cast. Then this intelligence can, without losing face, develop the inclination to look more closely at certain philosophical concepts as they exist in Rudolf Steiner's anthroposophy. To begin with, they can serve as working hypotheses. One there comes across the view that the idea of evolution so vigorously promoted by the newly emerging scientific studies of nature is also applicable to science itself, to human consciousness and to its potentialities in general. Modern scientific methods are given their due, but they, too, show their relativity inasmuch as their achievements — grandiose as they may be — reveal their one-sidedness. Only one plane of world-reality is being dealt with. But there are several such planes and, corresponding to them, several forms of human consciousness. Without the hypothesis that there are other methods of establishing reality, one can only see ignorance and fantasy in the old religions of a bygone humanity, although the cultural creations left behind by these 'unenlightened' people must make a deep impression. A different aspect presents itself the moment one considers the possibility that myths and fairy-tales are echoes of a clairvoyance that was originally inherent in human beings and gave them direct knowledge of the existence of supersensible worlds and beings. As long as the question is: 'How did religion come into being?' one gets nowhere. The question must be: 'How did it get lost?'

Anthroposophy speaks of a form of consciousness that is clearly defined as *imagination*. Images appear clairvoyantly, beheld directly as such, which must not, however, be made to relate to material matters; rather they should be seen as windows through which something supersensible can be glimpsed, something that has created in just this image an appropriate expression of itself. Visions of this kind were known in the old religions. They immediately become absurd if applied to material matters; if, for example, the hammer of Thor is taken for a material object. The fact that the idea of God held by different peoples varied considerably, does not mean that what they perceived was not reality; for the realms of supersensible beings should be thought of as a manifold abundance of hierarchically graded spirits who worked in different ways in the various cultures and religions.

The old way in which supersensible reality was perceived had something instinctive. It was lost to the degree to which humanity 'landed' with its consciousness on the material earth and developed a one-sided natural science based on sensory observations and the intellect. This consciousness works with enormous efficiency towards wakefulness and independence of the human being, but it completely loses sight of the supersensible reality, and is therefore quite incompetent to deal with religious contents. The necessary progress will be made only if the 'lost provinces' which had lain shrouded in twilight long before total darkness fell, are to be recovered for the knowledge of reality in a new way, by means of the newly-acquired wide-awake consciousness. In this direction — and not by looking back and reaching into the past for old practices — does anthroposophy wish to be understood. By making clear distinctions between the various stages of consciousness, and the spheres pertaining to them, it is in a position to do full justice to the old religions as well as to science. Such a distinction was not possible in former times.

Anthroposophy also presents us with the unique opportunity to comprehend Christianity. It is not one of the old religions depending on diminishing archetypal revelations. Here an event of the very highest order bursts into the history of humankind. To the question: what new reality was it then that the Christ brought, the answer would have to be: himself! He brought himself, a divine being who, through the deed of Golgotha, transposed himself into the sphere of earthly humanity in order to help it by his supersensible presence to enter now, in freedom and independence, into the New Covenant with the world of its origin. The Christ is not one of the founders of a religion, and his deed of redemption can be made to stand side by side only with the creation of the world itself as the next continuing chapter, as has been shown in the prologue to John's gospel.

The gospels tell of this Christ-event which unfolds between the Baptism in the Jordan and Golgotha. Interwoven with these happenings are major and minor supersensible elements, and the gospels can only be understood against a background of a philosophy that restores to the supersensible its rightful place as a reality.

In the field of gospel research, modern science has gathered together any number of items that, under the heading of 'background,' were intended to assist comprehension. But absent was 'expert knowledge' in the true sense, a knowledge that enables one to approach the 'question of truth.'

An example: modern theology accepts that the question of 'heaven opening' at the Baptism in the Jordan has now been finally demythologized and 'disposed of' by modern astronomy, not to mention astronautics, because 'in reality' there is only a black void. Similarly, the 'descent' of the dove is lost. From where is it supposed to have descended? And, anyway, what do 'above' and 'below' mean? If one can accept that 'imagination' exists, then these images found in the gospels can stand as statements of truth. They are visions. Made to relate to the material plane, they become absurd. But as visionary images they are a legitimate expression of the fact that by taking possession of Jesus, a being from the supersensible world entered the earthly world. Superstition only arises where reference is made to the wrong plane; then it is easy to demolish such images.

And when in the narrative of the Jordan Baptism a heavenly voice sounds forth, it is worth listening to what anthroposophy has to say about a second state of consciousness beyond that of imagination, which is called *inspiration*. Just as imagination is related to seeing, so inspiration is related to hearing; it opens to the soul's devoted listening — a hearing that is able to surrender completely to its object. In the same way as the visionary image can be clothed in pictorial forms that exist already in the 'inventory' of the soul (such as 'heaven,' or 'dove'), so inspiration appearing as inner persuasion, can be clothed in language available at any given time, and use words that are already waiting in the soul.

This type of study should satisfy the need for 'interpretation' that found voice in the demythologization theory. An abstract philosophy which does not consider the possibility of a consciousness extended to encompass the supersensible, cannot accomplish the interpretation demanded here. It can only eliminate all that does not conform to the materialistic view of the world. Instead of interpreting, it can only 'dispose of.'

Included in these 'disposed-of' subject matters is the Transfiguration narrative which we shall look at more closely in the following pages.

The Transfiguration on the mountain

Rudolf Bultmann has no doubt that the Transfiguration narrative is a 'legend.' Although — and this should be food for thought — it is chronologically bound up with another important event in all three gospels, namely the confession of Peter. With a stroke of the pen Bultmann simply shifts it to an entirely different point in time. According to him, Peter's confession,

> like the Transfiguration of Jesus, is an Easter story
> projected back into the life of Jesus by Mark (Mark
> 9:2-8). Legend is the account of the baptism of Jesus
> (Mark 1:3-10) and this is as certain as that the legend
> rests on the historical fact of the baptism of Jesus by
> John. It has not been told in the interest of biography
> but in the interest of religious faith, and it is an account
> of the consecration of Jesus as the Messiah. It dates
> from the time when the life of Jesus was already re-
> garded as Messianic while the Transfiguration, being
> the original Resurrection story, dates his Messianity
> back from the Resurrection. Legend also is the Tempta-
> tion story ...*

The appearance of the Risen One before Peter 'is reflected in the narratives of Peter's acknowledgement of the Messiah, of the Transfiguration ...'

Because there are certain suggestions reminiscent of the Easter narratives, it has simply been decreed that Peter's confession and the Transfiguration are 'backdated Easter stories.' Before embarking on such enormous changes one really ought to begin by taking the gospels for the phenomena which they present in themselves, look at them as such and see where the actual text leads us.

The idea of the Transfiguration being a legend does not

---

* *Theologie des Neuen Testamentes,* p.28.

accord very well with the fact that it appears to be connected with the striking event of Peter's confession by a very accurate chronological statement. Except for the account of the Holy Week, the Synoptic Gospel writers use no such built-in chronology anywhere. A legend floats in a chronologically indeterminate space, whereas the Transfiguration is expressly tied to the course of events at a specific point in time. Of course, according to Bultmann, Peter's confession, too, would have been 'backdated,' belonging in reality to Easter. This is contradicted, among other things, by the fact that according to Matthew and Mark this confession is, in its turn, tied to a place specifically identified: Caesarea Philippi. Nowhere else is this place mentioned in the New Testament; it lies far to the north in Palestine, close to the Mount Hermon ranges. Nowhere is it said that this place was of any importance at the time of the manifestations of the Risen Christ. Neither has the name any symbolic significance that could have led to Peter's confession having been shifted to just there. There is no reason to doubt this positive identification of a place. Nor has the narrative any legendary features and nothing miraculous happens. And into precisely this event the Transfiguration is locked, chronologically.

Incidentally, the chronological link also applies to the following: All three Synoptic Gospel writers have their report of the possessed boy whom the disciples who had stayed behind were unable to heal, closely follow that of the descent from the Transfiguration mountain. According to Luke 'the next day' (9:37).

The Transfiguration narrative exists in three versions, as does Peter's confession recorded by the so-called 'Synoptic' gospel writers, Matthew, Mark and Luke.

For specific reasons the following study will begin with the last of the three texts, that of Luke.

Luke shows a special sensitivity to the spiritual significance of an event. More than Matthew or Mark, he gives us the 'psychological' points of contact for an initial understanding of the supersensible events described. While Matthew, in speaking of the transformation of Jesus into a glorious sunlike being, simply includes it in his text, Luke speaks of the praying of Jesus, out of which develops what follows. He hints at what the disciples feel, so that through his account we can gain a much more intimate insight into the whole incident.

We are thus in a much better position to approach the more cosmically attuned account of Matthew that provides a certain polarity to Luke's report (like inside-outside). Then we can also deal with the less obvious characteristics of Mark's version.

18. According to Luke

As already mentioned, the Transfiguration is preceded by the confession of Peter. In Luke we do not read anything about the scenery, geographically so distinctive. He does not mention the walk to the north or the name Caesarea Philippi. Instead he gives an indication of the inner situation from which develops all that follows.

The question put to the disciples

'Now it happened that, as he was praying alone, the disciples were with him: and he asked them: who do the people say that I am ...? And who do you say that I am?' (9:18-20). This momentous question represents a turning-point. From here on the course of events flows ever faster towards the mystery of Golgotha.

It is characteristic of Luke's account that he speaks of the Christ's solitary praying out of which the question arises. 'He was praying,' meaning an extended period of time.

From being deep in prayer, the Christ turns to the disciples and asks the question. In this question, then, there is nothing incidental or accidental. It arises out of deeper connections. Peter answers with his confession to the *Christ of God* (9:20).

The Christ gives to this great word the concrete content belonging to it: with the *first announcement of the Passion.* The Synoptic Gospel writers agree that there were three such specific, solemn predictions of the Golgotha mystery, and that the first one was made immediately after Peter's confession. For the first time Christ speaks openly and directly of the approaching violent death and subsequent resurrection. Luke omits the protest of Peter who would keep the suffering from the Christ, and immediately proceeds to Christ's *invitation to follow him.* It is a characteristic feature of the redemptive deed of Golgotha that those to be redeemed should be included in its dynamic as 'sufferers with Christ, dying ones, resurrected ones.' — Finally, the vision extends to the Second Coming: *when the Son of Man shall come ...* (9:26).

The transition to the Transfiguration

After the word of the Second Coming the Christ begins to speak once more: 'But I tell you truly' (9:27). Then follows the saying about 'some standing here who will not taste death before they see the Son of Man coming in his kingdom' — so says Matthew. (Mark: 'The kingdom of God has come with power.' Luke: 'The Kingdom of God.')

Faced with such a prediction, one may be quick to point out that in fact it did not come true. One is inclined to regard it as a cheap apologetic explanation when some of the Early Fathers quite positively identified *some standing here* as the three disciples whom the Christ took with him to the Transfiguration event. In their vision of the transfigured Christ the promise was fulfilled. Thus Ephraem the Syrian says in his sermon on the Transfiguration: 'The men of whom he said that they would not taste death before they had beheld the preview of his coming, are those he took with him and led up the mountain. He showed them how he would come on Judgment Day in the magnificence of his divinity and the body of humanity.'

In order to do justice to such an assertion one must take into account a spiritual law of progression which John expresses in the sentence: 'It will *be* and already *is.*' In spiritual perception a series of future events widely spaced in their 'real' progression can appear contracted into a single image. The gospels mention 'the Day of the Son of Man,' but Luke has a passage where this 'day' is segmented into a series of 'days': 'The days are coming when you will desire to see one of the days of the Son of Man' (17:22). Thereby the Second Coming assumes space in time, and one can imagine the coming supersensible perception of the Christ already present, occurring in stages of gradually intensifying illumination of consciousness. What the disciples are allowed to see on the mountain is already in line with the events of the Second Coming. They anticipate something that shines into their souls as an 'and is already now.'

Moreover it should not be overlooked that all three Synoptic Gospel writers have the sentence about 'some standing here' followed immediately by the naming of the disciples whom the Christ takes with him to the mountain. A structural order such as this also has something to say. That certain perceptions can be expressed 'without words' by these means is readily observable in the gospels.

Eight days later

> Now about eight days after these sayings he took with
> him Peter and John and James and went up into the
> mountain to pray. (9:28).

The 'six days' Matthew and Mark speak of, and Luke's 'about eight days' do not necessarily contradict each other. Six days it is, if only the days between events are counted; eight, if the day of Peter's confession and the day of the Transfiguration are included. So it works out the same. And yet, the number eight preferred by Luke adds another nuance. Observation shows that Luke pays particular attention to the progress of events in time. In both his childhood chapters he mentions the period of growth from conception to birth (1:57; 2:6). He speaks of Elizabeth's fifth and sixth month (1:24-26), of the forty days of purification (2:22), of the twelve-year-old (2:42), of the anxious three-day search for the boy Jesus (2:46), of the thirty-year-old (3:23), of the forty days in the desert (4:2) and later, in the Acts, of the forty days to Ascension (1:3) and the fifty days to Whitsun (2:1). He speaks of the crippled woman's eighteen years of infirmity (13:11-16) and of Hannah's eighty-four years (2:37). In the childhood chapters we also come across the number eight. On the eighth day after birth the feast of circumcision and naming is celebrated for John (1:59) and Jesus (2:21) as 'octave' to the event of their birth. After conclusion of the seven-day week, the recurring event of a time-octave occurs, just as later the octave of the Easter day was experienced every Sunday, beginning with the first Sunday after Easter when the resurrected Christ appears before Thomas (John 20:26). Similarly, Luke makes the connection of the 'octave' at the beginning of the Transfiguration narrative, between the day of 'these words' and the later day when they were confirmed by the vision.

Christ's praying

Luke is in a special sense the evangelist of prayer. The first image Luke's gospel presents is of the priest Zechariah making the incense offering in the interior of the Temple, while the devout community outside accompanies the deed with their prayer. It is as if this incense-scented prayer was permeating the entire gospel of Luke's which, at its conclusion, leads us back into the Temple. 'And they worshipped him and returned to Jerusalem in great joy, and they were continually in the Temple praising and glorifying God' (24:53). In relation to the Jordan Baptism, Luke — and only Luke — mentions the praying of Jesus, which here, too, is of crucial significance. *It happened when ... Jesus also had been baptized and was praying, the heaven was opened.* (3:21). Soon after Jesus had begun his public activity, it says: *He withdrew into the wilderness and prayed* (5:16; also Mark 1:35). And yet another peculiarity of Luke: the ascent up the mountain, prior to the choosing of the twelve apostles, is for him the elevation to a great nocturnal prayer. 'He went up into the mountain to pray, and all night he continued in prayer to God' (6:12).

Not much later it says: 'He was praying in a certain place, and when he ceased, one of his disciples said to him: Lord, teach us to pray ...' (11:1). Then the Lord's Prayer, in a shorter version than we know it from Matthew, is given to the disciples. Matthew has built it into the great edifice of his Sermon on the Mount, still early in the gospel. Luke tells — at a later point in time — of a specific situation when this prayer was given to the disciples in answer to the request of one of them. Viewed merely historically, this version would seem to deserve being given preference. But both have their value: the way of Luke, to leave the words of the Christ within the framework of the particular situation as it occurred, and, on the other hand, the way of Matthew who makes larger compositions of connected sayings. Luke has preserved for us the situation surrounding the gift of the Lord's Prayer: once again the Christ was in one of his prayer-seclusions. But through Luke we learn that such a sustained contemplation could also be interrupted by an 'interval,' and in one of those intervals an unnamed disciple, apparently under the deep impression of this prayer, voiced the request that was granted so wonderfully. The Christ gives them the Lord's Prayer in its first form; the fully expanded seven-fold version which we know from the Sermon on the Mount (Matt.6:9-13), the Christ would have developed from there.

The transfigured countenance

While he prayed, *through* the act of praying, the transfiguring process began. Thereby Luke gives an important clue to a possible, at least rudimentary understanding, that the Transfiguration is not a miracle to be accepted 'from outside.' General inner human access to insight is available — in prayer. Initial experiences in this area are within the scope of what is, in general terms, humanly possible. It is only that the Christ has in an infinitely heightened measure what anyone who really prays can experience intuitively as inner illumination. But before Luke speaks of something like a higher light-substance bursting forth, he speaks of the Christ's countenance. *And as he was praying the visionary image of his countenance became different* (9:29). What we describe as 'visionary image' is in Greek *eidos.* This is a word that even in those days had already had a long history.

In Plato *eidos* stands for 'idea,' next to the Greek *idea.* *Idein* is 'seeing.' Hence, our idea is something one sees, something seen; but looked at closely, seeing not with the physical, but with the spiritual eye. The 'idea' is grasped in the beholding. Aristotle did not want to think of the idea as floating above things; as 'entelechy' he tried to link it more intimately with the world of the physical. Inasmuch as ente-lechy gives form to matter, he also called it *morphē,* 'form,' or else *eidos:* that which imagines the form for matter. The shape in which the forming power of the spiritual is revealed, discernible to the outer as well as the inner eye, is for Aristotle the *eidos.*

And now, at the Transfiguration, it is the *eidos* of the countenance which is seen. A human face is a very special object for the eye to behold. It is the strongest manifestation in the physical world of an inherently supersensible quality. Something of the spirit and of the soul can be looked at with the physical eye, as it were. Physical eye and spiritual eye come together almost completely. The 'visage' visible to the physical eye is, at the same time, 'vision' to spiritual perception. The human visage is truly a vision.

Of this *eidos* of the countenance of Jesus, Luke says that it became 'different' — *heteron* — while he prayed. One might wonder at this expression which apparently says so little. Could it be something like a deliberate understatement — the use of all too modest a word because, in any case, even eloquent speech cannot come close to what has to be said. Or how else could it be understood? For 'different' there are two Greek terms: *allos* and *heteros*. *Allos* is a more general term for change. There are also versions of the text which use the verb *alloioō* here: 'the appearance was altered.' But the reading 'became different *[heteron]*' is still preferable, one would think. In *heteros* can be divined the significance of the difference, of the strangeness created by the difference. In comparison one could perhaps think of impressions created by the sight of a dying person. Suddenly something hitherto unknown mingles with the familiar features, something alienating infusing them with unapproachable majesty. We feel, here is not only the human being as we knew him or her in everyday life. The unselfconscious familiarity bred by daily contact gives way to a solemn feeling which divines the eternal being that up to this moment has been hidden in the physical substance. An experience of this kind, a groping for distance-creating majesty, would be at the back of Luke's word 'different,' which sounds so reserved.

The possibility would also have to be considered that the Transfiguration on the Mountain is indeed connected with something like an approach to the threshold of death. If this be accepted as a possibility, then much that is enigmatic in the gospels appears in a new light. One can begin to perceive why the Christ walks towards his death in Jerusalem with such certitude, why he 'wanted to die at the Passover.' He wanted to accomplish his death, awaiting him in any case, in the form of the Golgotha mystery as death on the cross, as had been intended in spirit. He wanted to 'fulfil what had been written,' not only in old books but, above all, written in the stars according to destiny's divine necessity. Hence the 'must' in the first announcement of the Passion — the Son of Man 'must' suffer and die. In Luke this 'must' reappears in the Emmaus narrative: 'Did not the Christ *have to* suffer these things to enter into his glory?' The events of the Holy Week, in particular from Maundy Thursday to Easter morning, are governed by the inner necessity of the 'must' to be complied with in freedom. At Golgotha, history and ritual coincide. To celebrate in this sense his last days before the end, suffering and aware, was the task that stood before the Christ. In his corporeality he had to hold in check the death that had begun to make itself known, until he would be free to say: 'It is accomplished.' Seen like this, the wrestling at Gethsemane appears in a new light. It is not that he flinches from the cross at the last moment after all, but that death threatens to carry him off before the appointed hour. The Transfiguration would then represent an important stage in the course of the confrontation with death. It is not accidentally flanked by the first and the second announcement of the Passion (9:22 and 9:44). Such an announcement is not only the communication of a thought, rather it springs from a real presentiment of death. In his call for followers, the Christ speaks for the first time of the 'cross' that has to be taken up (9:23; Luke adds 'daily'). There is no previous mention of the cross. Matthew has the word of 'the cross to be taken up' in an earlier passage (10:38), but it should be considered that he gathers specific sayings into large compositions, and in this case, too, a later saying was put into the earlier 'sending-out address.' At any rate, Mark as well as Luke has the word 'cross' appear for the first time *here*. And it does not yet refer directly to the cross of Golgotha arising, as it does, out of the Christ's own experience: that from now on he will 'daily' have to 'take upon himself,' with great conscious effort, the cross of his earthly body dedicated to death, and carry it towards the conclusion of the mystery to be accomplished.

Thus the Transfiguration also shows a touch of the experience of being close to death. On the mountain top, far removed from the world, the Christ enters into a spirit conversation with other souls dwelling 'in the beyond,' as if he were already dead. He could now 'pray himself out' of his body, as it were, and cross over to his divine spiritual home. The Transfiguration would then have been the beginning of a sublime dying process. The Christ contained his heavenly light-being just once more in his earthly-human form and came down from the mountain in order to accomplish his true, great mystery at Golgotha.

The glistening garments

Luke also speaks of garments which begin to glisten (9:29). This bursting forth of inner light is also for Luke the result of praying. The praying soul gathers and condenses that which lives in it as inner light. The more powerfully this process works, the better the soul-light can communicate with the delicate life-organism, finally showing its reflection even in the depths of the physical body.

'The light in you' — this is also spoken of in the gospels. Matthew has included it in his Sermon on the Mount. Luke has left this saying of Christ in its actual original position, not at the beginning, but only after the event of the Transfiguration. 'Be careful therefore lest the light in you be darkness' (11:35). In this very passage Luke, going beyond Matthew, has passed on something else, something very strange: 'If then your body is full of light *(phōteinon)* having no part dark, it will be wholly lightlike, as when a lamp flashes its rays through you' (11:36). This saying quite obviously rests on the fact of the Transfiguration having preceded it — indeed, it all but arises from it. The inner source of the light illuminates *(phōtizei)* like a flash of lightning the whole human being, penetrating to the very sheathlike nature of his body.

A comprehensive way of looking at the gospels that takes note of the consonances will reveal the remarkable fact that this term, 'flash,' is reminiscent of Luke's description of the garments beginning to glisten as part of the transfiguration process. The garments turned white, 'flashing forth' *(ex-astraptōn)*. Luke also speaks of the 'flashing' robe of the two Easter angels at the tomb (24:4). What is the specific note that thereby comes into the description of Luke?

A 'lightning flash' is 'light in motion.' Not a light in repose, but one creating itself in activity. Of this nature is the radiance that emanates from the two angels at the tomb; of this nature is the light that emanates from the praying Christ, penetrating his garments, as it were, and completely enveloping him. It is a light alive in itself, a light of a higher order that cannot, any other time, be experienced in an earthly context.

In connection with the Transfiguration, this 'flashing' is now combined with 'forth' — 'flashing forth.' In all of the New Testament it is found only here, in Luke's gospel. In the description of the two Easter angels it is not used, although their light, too, alive with spiritual creativity, is called a 'flashing' one. The 'forth' points indirectly to an 'inwardness' that is the source of the phenomenon — the inwardness of the Christ become human, gathering his inner light in prayer.

The two spirit figures

While Matthew and Mark introduce Moses and Elijah without any preparation, simply saying 'there appeared to them ...,' and immediately calling them by name, Luke does it differently. Again we notice in him a sensitive awareness of the manner in which a supersensible experience takes shape, step by step, in the souls of the disciples. He does not immediately speak of 'Moses' and 'Elijah' — 'And behold two men talking with him ...' (Luke 9:30).

The 'behold' points to a perception unexpectedly presented to the spiritual eye. But what is revealed to this eye is initially only 'two men' who apparently have been talking with the Christ for some time ('they talked with him' is, in Greek, the imperfect tense). Roused by the jolt of the 'behold,' the disciples become conscious of an event that is already under way. By adding only now 'which were Moses and Elijah,' Luke allows participation in the next step: the two figures are recognized as Moses and Elijah. In a kind of inspiration the disciples become aware of the two names.

Only now does he say *'who appeared in glory'* (9:31). In recording Christ's word of the return of the Son of Man, which precedes the Transfiguration, all three Synoptic Gospel writers speak of the 'glory.' But only Luke takes up this word again in the Transfiguration narrative, mentioning it twice. Moses and Elijah 'appear in glory.' Immediately afterwards: 'The disciples saw his [the Christ's] glory' (9:32). The glory belongs to all three participants in this spirit conversation. By the process of dividing the glory of the Second Coming in a triune way — as glory of himself, the Father and the holy angels, Luke creates a delicate relationship, weaving back and forth between the two sets of trinities. In the Old Covenant Moses re-establishes the connection back to the beginning. He beholds the genesis and accepts the law designed to keep the world on course as envisaged by creation. In contrast, Elijah was felt to be the genius of prophecy around whom blazes eschatology and apocalypse. He points to the future. Thus the light-aura of Moses contains something of the 'glory of the Father,' that of Elijah something of the 'glory of the Holy Spirit,' whose angel-messengers very much include Elijah. Between these two figures stands the Christ, the Son, 'in the glory of himself,' even though it will not be exalted to its full majesty before the great mystery of Golgotha has been accomplished.

The spirit conversation

The fact of these three holding a 'conversation' is perceived straight away. When the two are recognized as Moses and Elijah in their glory, the supersensible perception expands once more, in that something of the content of the conversation becomes intelligible. 'They spoke with him of his departure which he was to accomplish in Jerusalem' (9:31). This event was preceded by the first announcement of the Passion. Now it is being confirmed out of the higher knowledge of the great departed. These inhabitants of a higher world apparently look down with great interest to see what is happening to the one who has become flesh. They follow from above the course of his life on earth and are able to foresee prophetically the events taking shape at Jerusalem. They speak to the Christ of the 'departure' which signifies the end of his earthly path. The structure of what was to come, decreed by destiny, is already discernible to the consciousness of these spirits. And what has been foreseen must soon be fulfilled by means of actual earthly human experience and suffering.

There can be no doubt that Luke believes the two spirit beings to be the real individualities of Moses and Elijah who, after their departure from earth, continue to live in a higher world. He does not subscribe to the view that, until the time they are raised on the Day of Judgement, the dead are non-existent and simply 'quite dead.' This also becomes apparent from Luke's account of the story concerning the rich man and poor Lazarus (16:19-31), where after-death experiences of discarnate beings are described quite concretely to show how they may vary, depending on the life on earth that went before. There it is shown that discarnate beings can recognize each other, remembering events experienced together on earth, and are able to communicate with each other. Between the rich man and Father Abraham a 'spirit conversation' develops. The term 'parable' is not used at all for this story, it being a description of after-death conditions, taken from real life. Further, it is Luke who has the very word from the cross that presupposes a continuing life of the discarnate soul: 'Today you shall be with me in Paradise' (23:43). In like manner the appearance of Moses and Elijah as spirit beings of a higher order, manifesting themselves in 'glory' in the radiant light of a halo, are accepted as spiritually quite realistic.

The spirit conversation which has become perceptible to the disciples has the 'departure' as its subject. Departure — *exodos*

— is an important word. It combines *ex* with *hodos* — way. In the New Testament it is found only twice more, and in the gospels only here. In the Letter to the Hebrews (11:22) it describes the departure from Egypt, that is, the classical 'Exodus,' and in the Second Letter of Peter (1:15) Peter's impending death is defined as 'departure' from the tabernacle of his body. The death of Golgotha would also be what first comes to mind on reading Luke's words: 'accomplishing his departure from Jerusalem.' After all, 'accomplishing' is a bringing to an end. What was intended in the spirit becomes historical fact. To that extent 'exodos' is here, in the spirit conversation, the 'end of the way.' But not quite. The way on earth has run out, but opening up at the same time is the 'way out.' Thus, the end is given a new beginning. 'Exodus,' then, is the departure from an existing condition, an emerging and entering new territory. 'Exodus,' as defined here, can almost be termed a biblical 'leitmotif,' starting with Abraham's departure from Chaldea and the exodus of the tribes of Israel from Egypt (which provides the subject for the Book of Exodus) to the departure of God's people from the toppling Babylon of the Apocalypse (18:4). When the Christ's two heavenly interlocutors interpret the approaching Golgotha event as 'exodus,' then surely the tragic death motif also contains a promising hint of the 'exodus.' It is the reference to the new territory which the Christ, passing through the gate of death, will enter. As one who has died, who has risen from the dead and ascended to heaven, he will continue to be on the move in the grand manner. The Departed One wanders through the realm of the dead (1Pet.3:19). The Risen One says of himself: 'I am ascending to my Father,' (John 20:17). The Emmaus narrative of Luke who, in a special sense, is the evangelist of 'being on the move,' shows the Resurrected One as a wanderer. Nor does his ascension put an end to this movement the Christ is engaged in. The image of 'sitting on the right of the Father' does not necessarily exclude movement and activity. There can exist a lively activity that springs from an inner core of stillness. The Apocalypse contains both images: the Christ sitting on the throne (3:21), and the Christ walking (2:1). He wants those who belong to him to become 'wanderers with him' (3:4), to be on the move with him towards the far goal which is envisaged at the end of the Apocalypse as 'heavenly Jerusalem.'

In the spirit conversation the name of *Jerusalem* is heard also as the place of impending accomplishment. Surely this cannot be an accidental place reference in the manner of 'accidental historic truth' which is known in advance by prophetic spirits. The mystery to be accomplished cannot take place at any arbitrarily chosen locality. Jerusalem is a providential place. Jesus carries the certain knowledge in his soul that he will not die anywhere else but in Jerusalem (Luke 13:33). The third and most concrete announcement of the Passion begins with: 'Behold, we are going up to Jerusalem' (18:31).

Again it is necessary to look at Luke's gospel as a whole in order to see in its true light the name of Jerusalem as spoken by spirit mouths in so solemn a context. Of the three Synoptic Gospel writers Luke is the one to have a certain affinity to John, in that he develops a much stronger 'Jerusalem consciousness' than either Matthew or Mark. Jerusalem has a certain importance for Luke. It is very obvious in the two childhood chapters where three of the seven stories told unfold in the temple of Jerusalem. Quite some time before Palm Sunday we hear the call: 'Oh Jerusalem, Jerusalem, how often would I have gathered your children together' (13:34). 'How often ...' — then the Christ must have entered Jerusalem earlier — not only at the end, in the Holy Week. In the narrative of Simeon and Anna mention is made of a circle of apocalyptically-minded people 'who were looking for the redemption of Jerusalem' (2:38). In the Mount of Olives Apocalypse the destruction of the city is prophesied in concrete images (21:20–24). The Christ weeps for the city as he enters (19:41), and on his death-walk he bemoans the 'daughters of Jerusalem' (23:28).

Above all, however, it should be noted that Luke places the whole rich content of chapters 9:51–19:28 within the framework of the 'journey to Jerusalem,' thereby placing it under a specific sign. This walk begins with the solemn sentence: 'When the days drew near for him to be received up, he set his face to go to Jerusalem' (9:51). In two further passages (13:22 and 17:11) we are specifically reminded that whatever was recorded happened on the way to Jerusalem, in other words that it represents the sequence of stations along a 'path.' Luke is the one evangelist who, in his Easter narrative, takes account only of Jerusalem (Emmaus not being far distant). He alone has the Risen One mention the name of Jerusalem (24:47; also Acts 1:4 and 8). The disciples are to wait 'in the city' for the Pentecostal Spirit (24:49). Finally, one of the last sentences of the gospel says: 'And they returned to Jerusalem ...' (24:52).

In the consonance of all these passages the name of Jerusalem wants to be heard when it rings out in the spirit conversation at the Transfiguration. It is the earthly place for the mystery of Golgotha, the end of the road on earth for the One Incarnated in the Flesh, while above the earthly city there shines the apocalyptic gleam of the heavenly Jerusalem to which the Risen One is on his way.

The changing consciousness of the disciples

Luke is not concerned only with the conversation of the exalted three. He has also something to say about the state of soul the disciples experience during these events. 'Now Peter and those that were with him were heavy with sleep, and when they wakened they saw his glory and the two men who stood with him' (9:32).

The heaviness of sleep is reminiscent of Gethsemane. Doubtless more is involved than mere physical drowsiness. At Gethsemane the inner forces of vigilance fail the disciples when they are confronted with an extraordinary task that arose then. The 'agony' of the Christ has already been mentioned, and so has the task of the disciples to help him, who was prematurely threatened by death, to hold on to his failing physical body until the mystery could be accomplished. The disciples did not rise to the occasion as the hour demanded. They were not able to prevail against the superior force of the numbness and darkness that rose up out of the as yet untransformed earthly heaviness of their being. The 'power of darkness' of which the Christ speaks when he is taken prisoner (22:53) also has the effect of oppressive 'heaviness.' Matthew says that 'their eyes were made heavy' (26:43), and Mark 'weighed down' *(katabarynómenoi,* 14:40). Except in Luke, this word 'make heavy' *(barynō)* does not appear again anywhere else in the gospels. In the Mount of Olives Apocalypse the Christ unfolds the eschatological perspective in relation to his return, exhorting the disciples at the same time: '... take heed to yourselves lest your hearts be weighed down, be it with surfeit of food and drink, be it with nagging cares of this life' (Luke 21:34). The heart as a sunlike Christ-organ should be spiritually awakened, but opposing this is the darkening power of 'heaviness.'

The Christ took the three disciples up the Mountain of Transfiguration because the elevation of the mountain predisposes towards the experience of light and spiritual 'lightness.' As darkness and heaviness belong together, so too do light and lightness.

The failure of the disciples, here on the mountain, is not as total as that at Gethsemane. Luke uses quite a unique, concretely spiritual expression: *diagrēgorēsantes* which would have to mean: 'awakening in between.' Obviously it is a question of moments of wakefulness flashing into the heaviness of sleep. In such bright moments of higher consciousness which the disciples manage to achieve nevertheless, *'they see his glory.'* That we are dealing with supersensible perception is shown also by a passage in the Second Epistle of Peter.

There the Mountain of Transfiguration is called the 'holy mountain' *(hagion oros)*, and for the disciples the technical mystery term *epoptai* is used, which is known from the Eleusinian mysteries (2Pet.1:18,16).

The disappearance of the two spirit figures

Luke then describes how this image begins to dissolve. *'And it happened as they departed from him ...'* (9:33). The space involved in 'near' and 'far' is not something purely physical in a context like this one. When in the Easter narrative of Matthew the Risen One 'approaches' the disciples 'some of whom' still 'doubt' (28:17), this manifestly points to a heightened intensity of his self-revelation. He makes an effort to reveal himself still more clearly to the limited visionary powers of his disciples. He makes a movement 'towards them.' Here, in the Transfiguration, the opposite happens. The spirit event with Moses and Elijah has passed its zenith and a reversal of movement ensues, a fading of the impression. Thus Moses and Elijah are engaged in a movement that takes them from the sphere of manifestation back into the depths of the world of God. They distance themselves and the distance grows.

This special feature of Luke's account can also assume still more eloquence for us if we take note of the consonance once more. It is not the only time that Luke, when writing about a spiritual event, considers it worth while to describe the ending, the way it concludes. Thus, Gabriel's annunciation to Mary ends with: 'And the angel departed from her' (1:38). And in the Christmas story: 'And when the angels had gone away from them [the shepherds] into heaven ...' (2:15). At the Emmaus manifestation the Risen One becomes invisible at the moment of being recognized *(aphantos egeneto,* 24:31). Ascending to heaven, the Christ 'removes himself' *(diéstē)* from the disciples while blessing them (24:51). This vanishing

from sight Luke describes in even more detail in the Acts
(1:9). Occasionally the departure of an angel who had appeared
is also described in the Acts (10:7; 12:10).

In this manner Luke describes how the two figures begin
their retreat from visibility. And for Luke this is exactly the
'psychological' moment when one of the disciples, Peter, utters
his words: 'And as the men were parting from him, Peter said
to Jesus "Master, it is well that we are here; let us make three
tabernacles, one for you, one for Moses and one for Elijah" —
not knowing what he said.' (9:33). Peter feels the bliss
connected with a spirit encounter. Peter wants to hold what is
about to vanish. There comes to him the image of 'building a
tabernacle.' It could have been the time when the Feast of
Tabernacles was approaching. Peter would like to provide a
place to stay for the three, wanting to transform 'being' in a
higher world into 'staying.'

Entering the cloud

The words of Peter, not spoken out of an alert consciousness,
are soon overtaken by a further progression of the supersensible event. 'And as he said this, a cloud came and overshadowed them; and they were afraid as they entered the cloud.'
(9:34).

That a cloud forms around a mountain peak is a natural phenomenon. However, there is something special about this
cloud. In the Old Testament the cloud concealing Mount Sinai
carries the presence of God. A cloud takes away the Christ
ascending to heaven. In the clouds of heaven, it is said, the
Second Coming will occur. The cloud appearing at the Transfiguration is also a Revelation phenomenon. All three Synoptic
Gospel writers speak of the disciples being 'overshadowed' by
the cloud. Luke's account in particular is reminiscent of 'Mary
being overshadowed by the Holy Spirit' (1:35). Luke's account
immediately resumes its own direction: 'And they were afraid

as they entered the cloud.' If the text were referring to the disciples entering, one would have to imagine that they themselves were touched by the descending cloud. Since the cloud is the vehicle of a divine presence — it is from the cloud that the voice is heard later on — the 'fear' of the disciples, as they entered the cloud, would have had its origin in the shock experienced by earthly human beings coming into direct contact with a higher reality. They would feel their own inadequacy and would be alarmed at the approaching threshold of a higher existence.

This being afraid, however, would also make sense in our text if it meant: 'as those — Moses and Elijah — entered the cloud.' The 'fear' of the disciples would then be the devout awe with which they witnessed a 'communion' of human spirits with the divine. The witnessing of such happenings is enough to bring the threshold-shock before the soul of the disciples still incarnated in the physical body. Moses and Elijah had come out of their life 'in God' into a manifestation directed towards the earth, and now the hour has passed and they returned to their state of 'communion' with the divine.

The voice of heaven

'And a voice happened out of the cloud saying: this is my beloved Son. Him hear!' (9:35). *Egeneto* — 'it happened.' This turn of phrase favoured by Luke in other passages as well, returns with conspicuous frequency in the Transfiguration narrative. It lends emphasis to the event-character, the progression of happenings as they come into being (9:28,29,33,34,35). The voice from the cloud 'happens.' As the voice of God from above it represents the climax of the whole series of events. It is reported by all three Synoptic Gospel writers, although their accounts differ slightly. However, the reference to the voice heard by Jesus and John at the Jordan Baptism is unmistakable in all three accounts. 'Thou art my beloved Son, this day have I begotten thee.' (3:22).

This great begetting formula as told in its true version by Luke, enhances even further the significance of the Jordan Baptism. What happens 'this day' of eternity between Father and Son as thou and I, radiates into the temporal 'this day' of the Jordan Baptism. The process of begetting the Son descends into Jesus of Nazareth. Distinctly at variance with this is the cloud-word spoken at the *Transfiguration.* This time it is not a direct begetting event. It is not directed at the Son. It is not framed in the second person of the 'thou.' Rather, speaking in the third person, it is directed as a kind of 'demonstration' at the disciples, as at 'third parties' who now shall have their share of perceiving the mystery. Hence, this time it does not say: 'thou art,' but 'this is.' Peter's confession of the week before, sensing but not yet knowing, finds its full divine confirmation here. At the Jordan Baptism John the Baptist too heard the divine word in a kind of 'attendant consciousness' from the perspective of earthly humanity. Into this attendant consciousness the disciples were now to enter.

Luke's version of the cloud-word addressed to the disciples also differs from that of Matthew and Mark. With him it is not 'beloved' Son, but 'chosen' — *eklelegménos.* In the choosing, *eklegō,* however, we may also hear the *legō,* the speaking, the *logos.* It is the Son 'pronounced' by the Father in a very deep sense. Here too a certain closeness to John is noticeable in Luke.

Thereby the concluding words also assume additional depths. 'Him hear!' Surely this is not only an exhortation directed at faithful pupils to listen to the sayings of their teacher. It was hardly something that had to be recommended to pupils of a Jewish rabbi of that time. Attention and retention were strongly cultivated. The 'hearing' is not so much aimed at the individual sayings, as at 'him.' They should be open and receptive in their devotion to him as the Logos himself in the revelation of his very being.

Luke is the evangelist of 'hearing.' This has to do with the fact that in a special sense he could also be called the evangelist of the soul. In its highest potential the soul takes its image from Mary who, as the handmaiden of the Lord, devotes herself to the divine and becomes the Mother of God. The devoted hearing becomes an impregnating process on the highest level. The relationship of hearing to being mother is clearly recognizable with Luke. It is underlined once more by the episode where a woman from the crowd calls the mother of Jesus blessed for being the mother of such a son, and receives the reply: 'Rather blessed are they who hear the word of God and keep it.' (11:28). The Christ says in effect: You too can become my mother, inasmuch as I am the logos of God. Your soul too can become Mary.

The silence

With this climax of divine inspiration from out of the mysterious cloud, the whole series of supersensible events has reached its conclusion. In the echo of that 'Hear!' the transition to everyday consciousness is accomplished. 'And when the voice had happened, Jesus was found alone' (9:36). He stands before their eyes again in the guise of the rabbi of Nazareth.

And *'they kept silent and told no man in those days any of the things they had seen'* (9:36). Only Luke says that the disciples were silent 'of their own accord' *(autoi)*. Here he uses the solemn word *sigaō*. In the New Testament 'to be silent' is expressed with *sigaō* or *siōpaō*. The latter means more generally that speaking is suspended, nobody talks. The first means to be silent, not only with the lips but with the whole soul, a silence coming from inside. The noun *sigē* as mystery word is well known — for example in the Mithras liturgy *(Sigē! Sigē! Sigē!)*. At the end of the Letter to the Romans (16:25) Paul very solemnly speaks of the unveiling *(apocalypsis)* of the mystery 'which has been kept secret for aeons.' In the Apocalypse a 'silence lasting for half an hour' precedes the sounding of the seven trumpets (8:1).

In Luke's gospel the involuntary silence of Zachariah after his encounter with the angel is expressed with *siōpaō*. However, this silence, initially imposed from outside, becomes in the course of nine months, equalling the pregnancy of Elizabeth, an essentially holy silence out of which will be born, parallel to the birth of the boy John, the song of praise 'Benedictus' (1:68–79). In the Acts Luke uses *sigaō* as well as *sigē* as solemn silence where appropriate (12:17; 15:12; 21:40). Paul speaks of the silence of the community during divine service (1Cor.14:28, 30) and there, of course, *sigaō* is used.

The Transfiguration as the supersensible experience of a mystery is, according to Luke, confirmed by the holy mountain. Luke has nothing else immediately follow the Transfiguration report. He says nothing of the important conversation about Elijah and the Baptist which, according to Matthew and Mark, took place during the descent from the mountain. He allows the Transfiguration to flow into the silence and dissolve in it. He only takes up the thread of his narrative 'on the next day when they had come down from the mountain' (9:37).

19. According to Matthew

Caesarea Philippi

While Luke speaks of the Christ's solitary praying that precedes the momentous question he puts to the disciples at an unspecified locality, Matthew as well as Mark mentions the name of Caesarea Philippi. Thereby a geographic scenery is set, unusual, if not unique, in the gospels. It lies high in the north of Palestine, near the snow-covered Mount Hermon ranges which rise to a height of 2760 m, near the springs of the Jordan that tumble down as waterfalls to the valley below. The Hermon with its snow-reflected light stretches across the horizon, closing off Galilee towards the north.

Matthew gives the most comprehensive account of the events that took place at Caesarea Philippi. He has much to say about Peter. Peter's confession is given the widest exposure here. 'You are the Christ, the Son of the living God' (16:16). Calling Peter blessed, the Christ replies with the word about the rock ('You are Peter — the rock — and on this rock I will build my church ...') and the 'handing over of the keys.' Then follows, as with the other Synoptic Gospel writers, the first announcement of the Passion. Peter dares to object. The fact that the Christ also talks of the Resurrection slips past his soul unnoticed. But the prospect of the Christ having to suffer elicits his immediate protest. 'This must not happen to you.' Whereupon he, who had just been singled out as blessed, is rebuked in the strongest and sharpest terms as a seducing 'Satan' who is an affront *(skandalon)* to the Christ. All this is completely missing in Luke. Matthew is more radical than Mark in describing both the positive and the negative aspects.

The ascent

Truly, I say to you there are some standing here who will not taste death before they see the Son of Man coming in his kingdom. And after six days Jesus takes with him Peter and James and John, his brother, and brings them up alone to the top of a high mountain. (16:28–17:1).

Luke prefers the past tense for his narrative. Mark, with his inclination for the dramatic, the present, and Matthew, most of the time but not always, the past. By jumping into the present on certain occasions, he can lend emphasis to an event and give his narrative something like a jolt. It happens here, at the ascent up the mountain. The Christ 'takes with him' the three disciples (in contrast to Luke, Matthew as well as Mark puts James before his brother) and 'brings them up' — *anapherei* in Greek — literally, *he carries them up*. The same with Mark. The expression is strange. However, the nuance of such an unusual word ought not to be lost. The Luke version shows how the disciples, although chosen specifically in their trinity from the total circle of twelve, and no doubt equipped with special qualifications, were nevertheless able to cope with the event only imperfectly and had to wrestle with the dulling earthly heaviness of their being. The unusual *anapherei* may point to the same state of affairs in a different way. We are familiar with the linguistic usage of somebody spiritually carrying a fellow human being. Maybe there is a hint that, in wanting to lead the only three of the twelve disciples who could be considered at all towards the mountain experience, the Christ had to add 'carrying power' of his own, in order to bring the disciples to something approaching 'the level' of what was to come.

The word, taking on special significance, appears also in the Letter to the Hebrews. There, mention is made both of the Christ as the great high-priest and of his sacrifice. The Letter

to the Hebrews says that the high-priest of the Mosaic Covenant must 'carry up' sacrifices again and again for his own
sins and those of his people, but that the Christ as high-priest
in the tradition of Melchizedek 'carried himself up' in a single
offering sufficient once and for all (7:27). Subsequently, the
anapherō appears in connection with the sins of humanity. The
Christ, 'offered up once and for all, in order to carry up the
sins of many' (9:28). Here it has the meaning that by taking
them upon himself, the Christ deprives the consequences of sin
existing objectively in the spiritual world.

Is it not possible that the significance of the sacrifice also
pulses softly in the *anapherei* of the Transfiguration narrative?
In 'carrying up' the three disciples to an initial vision of his
divine being, the Christ brings at the same time something like
a first gift from a new humanity to the heavenly world.

He leads the disciples up the mountain by themselves,
kat'idian. The *kata monos,* mentioned in connection with Luke,
points to the inner permanent core of the ego. *Idios* stands for
essence. Removed from the world, the disciples are expected
to enter the sphere of the essence and the essential. *Kat'idian*
is used most frequently by Matthew: for the prayer solitude of
the Christ before the Feeding of the Five Thousand (14:13),
and again afterwards (14:23). For the rest, it appears in connection with teaching in the inner circle (17:19; 20:17; 24:3).

The high mountain

According to all three Synoptic Gospel writers, the Transfiguration takes place on a mountain. With Luke, it is simply the
mountain as the place of inner elevation. With Matthew and
Mark it is a 'high mountain' and, according to some versions,
a very high one. Being a member of a chain which runs
through the entire gospel of Matthew, his high mountain
assumes a significance of special quality. Viewed in totality,
there appear to be exactly seven mountains.

First, the mountain of temptation to dominate the world. Matthew seems to make a point of placing this temptation in third place: 'And the devil takes him up a very high mountain' (4:8). (Luke has this temptation in second place and there is no mention of a mountain, only: 'The devil led him up.') On this very high mountain, the tempter lets the Christ behold all the riches of the world. All this I will give you.

This first mountain of Matthew is balanced at the other end by that 'mountain in Galilee' on which (and we read this only in Matthew) the Risen One reveals himself to his disciples (28:6). He has not accepted world domination from the devil. He has walked the path of sacrifice and may now say: 'I have been given all the power in heaven and on earth.' The Easter mountain is the last of the seven mountains. A bow spans the distance between the first mountain and the seventh one.

The second mountain is the scene of the disciples' elementary instruction. 'When he saw the multitude he went up into a mountain and when he had sat down his disciples came to him and he opened his mouth and taught them' (5:1f). This is Matthew's Sermon on the Mount. Rising physically to the top of the mountain and reaching for the highest and ultimate goal of perfection — 'perfect as your Father in heaven is perfect' — this is harmony. In the Sermon on the Mount is heard for the first time a reference to the 'heavenly Father,' the 'Father in the heavens,' so characteristic of the gospel of Matthew. Incidentally, the Sermon on the Mount also contains a reference to the 'city on the mountain' (5:14).

This sermon mountain, the second in the series of seven, is mirrored by the sixth mountain which is also a mountain of spiritual instruction. On Tuesday evening of Holy Week, the Christ sits down on the Mount of Olives (24:3) and the disciples question him about his *parousia* and the conclusion of the aeon. He gives them the Mount of Olives Apocalypse and concludes with the image of the Last Judgement. Between these two teaching mountains a bow stretches from two to six within the sevenfoldness.

147

The three middle mountains are in the specific area of prayer and meditation and are connected with marvellous manifestions of power. Matthew mentions — in third place within the series of seven — the Christ's ascent 'up into a mountain apart to pray' (14:23). Out of this mountain prayer he allows himself to be seen by the disciples in supersensible form, coming to them as one walking on the lake, as they in their boat battle wind and waves. This manifestation is not unconnected with the praying on the mountain. In fourth place stands the mountain they ascend as a prelude to the Feeding of the Four Thousand (15:29). 'He came across the sea of Galilee and went up into a mountain and sat down.' Such a 'sitting down on the mountain' is without doubt an indication of meditation. The mountain force flows into the event taking shape, with the Christ praying down forces of heaven onto the bread and fishes. John's gospel also has a 'sitting down on the mountain' preceding the Feeding (6:3), giving it crucial significance. Matthew's fifth mountain is the high mountain of the Transfiguration (17:1) with its supersensible occurrences. That makes it deserving of a 'rating' within Matthew's composition of seven. Here too the sweep of a bow is discernible between the third and the fifth mountains. The walk on the lake which has the solitary mountain meditation as an essential prerequisite (Mark says that the praying figure on the mountain 'saw' the disciples in their boat battling the wind, and came to them), and the Transfiguration on the Mountain have this in common — that out of the mountain prayer a special opportunity arises for the Christ to manifest his supersensible being before the beholding disciples. The fourth mountain, with the Feeding of the Four Thousand, then comes to stand in the middle of the series of seven.

One could wonder if Golgotha, too, should not be included in this series of Matthew's mountains. Golgotha, however, is not described as a 'mountain' in any of the gospels, it being only a rocky hill. With Matthew, the sevenfoldness is certainly no more accidental than the seven parables of the lake. Mark mentions only four of the seven mountains: the mountain of the choosing of the disciples (3:13); the mountain of prayer before the walk on the lake (6:46); the mountain of Transfiguration (9:2, 9); and, in the Holy Week, the Mount of Olives (13:3) with the speech about last things. Luke speaks of three mountains: choosing of the disciples (6:12f), Transfiguration (9:28,37) and Mount of Olives, the last one also being called the overnight stopping place (21:37; 22:39). John limits himself to the mountain on which the Christ 'sat down' (6:3) and to which he retires again after the Feeding of the Five Thousand before the walk on the lake (6:15). He also mentions the Mount of Olives as overnight resting place during the autumn festival (8:1). Seen against the other gospels, Matthew's special relationship to mountains becomes obvious.

With the motif of the holy mountain Matthew also continues the line of the Old Testament — Morijah, Sinai-Horeb, Nebo, Garizim, Carmel, Zion. In each case the mountain is the place of 'higher' experience. It shows up very distinctly especially in the Sinai experience of Moses. On the mountain he accepts the law. On the mountain the cult for Israel was revealed to him. On the mountain, finally, Moses was granted a theophany: although not permitted to see God's countenance, he may, nevertheless, 'gaze after him' as he passes. Outer and inner elevation were inseparably joined for the people of old. On ascending a mountain one experienced a change in the state of soul, an opening up to the supersensible. The holy mountain is actually an archetypal, religio-spiritual experience common to all humanity.

Metamorphosis

Matthew's report now passes straight on to the Transfiguration event. 'And was transformed before them' (17:2) — *metemorphōthē*. The verb *metamorphoō* — metamorphose — is used in the gospels only here and in the parallel passage of Mark (9:2).

Apart from that, it appears in the New Testament only twice more, in the letters of Paul. 'You will be transformed by the renewing of your mind *(nous)'* (Rom.12:2). 'We are transformed into this same image, from glory to glory' (2Cor.3:18). This metamorphosis comes about through us 'reflecting with open face the glory of the Lord, as in a glass,' exposing ourselves to the streaming-in of his image in order that it may form and transform us. Paul also speaks of a gradual metamorphosis occurring step by step 'from glory to glory.' In the same letter Paul says: 'God who commanded the light to shine out of darkness, shone into our hearts to give us the light of knowledge of the glory of God in the face of Jesus Christ' (2Cor.4:6). In the countenance of the One become Man shines the glory of God, and Christians will share in this glory in progressive metamorphosis.

Paul describes the gradual transformation that took place in the Christening of the human being who looks with cognition towards the glory in the countenance of the Christ. The gospel describes the precondition for such a process: First the glory of God had to shine 'in the countenance of the Christ Jesus' in archetypal perfection. Matthew is the portrayer of this happening. His account contains the singular reference to the metamorphosis of an earthly human face into something sunlike — the quintessential metamorphosis.

The sun

And he was transformed before them, and his
countenance shone as the sun (17:2)

People of former times associated quite different experiences with looking at heavenly bodies than do people of the scientifically awakening modern times, let alone our space-age. The world-vision of former times was a 'physiognomical' one, as it were. Looking at a human face one is not primarily interested in the physical side of the phenomenon, but rather something non-physical, spiritual, that shows in the face in an immediately legible way. Anatomical, biological or chemical research would be an entirely different matter. It would be a departure from interpreting a face by 'runic reading' and lead to quite a different territory. For people of ancient times, sun, moon and stars were primarily an expression of their inherent spirituality. Paul still speaks of the different glories of the sun and the moon, and the specific individual glory of each single star (1Cor.15:41). Just as a personal psyche shines out of every human eye, so a different cosmic spirituality shines out of every heavenly body.

In olden times the state of consciousness would not even have allowed a separation of research methods. While the soul was turned beholding towards the cosmos, perception with the physical eye slid imperceptibly into visions of clairvoyant imagery. Thus, in the varying light of the heavenly bodies one could discern the emergence of various supersensible substantialities. The physically visible star-light triggered perception of the 'aura' of the star in question, the 'glory,' in Paul's words. One cannot do justice to the old star-cults if one does not concede them perceptions of this kind, at least as far as their origins are concerned. Beyond the cosmic corporeality of sun and moon there is yet something else, a strange qualitative characteristic, something sunlike and moonlike which has its representation in the heavenly body in question which, however, can also be found elsewhere in the world. Van Gogh was able to substitute the sun for the figure of Jesus in his copy of Rembrandt's *Raising of Lazarus*. He had the sensitivity for the 'sunlike.' Only if there is renewed recognition of such things can Christianity regain its 'cosmic dimensions.' To bring together the Christ and the sun would be an absurd beginning as long as one thinks of a Jewish reformist Rabbi on the one hand, and a glowing ball of fire on the other. But, according to Matthew, what the disciples perceive on the mountain is precisely this, that the sunlike in Jesus lives in a human way. Only if one arrives again at the ability to see something 'countenance-like' in the physical sun, in the sense of a 'physiognomic' world-contemplation, can one accept the full impact of the idea that the sun now shines again from a human face. On reading the sentence 'his countenance shone like the sun,' one will then no longer be satisfied with a non-committal poetic comparison. This passage, unique in the gospels, has its equal only in the Apocalypse of John. John beholds on the 'day of the Lord,' a Sunday, the day of the sun, the Risen One in his greatness. 'His countenance shone like the sun in his strength' (1:16).

Cosmic aspects in Matthew's writing

In Matthew's gospel one is frequently reminded of the spirituality of the cosmically disposed Zarathustra religion.

There are certain other *sun*-words. Mindful of the consonance, one may observe the fact that only in Matthew — in the Sermon on the Mount — a reference is found to the royal 'giving virtue' of the divinity who generously 'makes his sun rise on the evil and the good' (5:45). Equally, only Matthew has preserved the saying of 'the righteous who will shine forth like the sun in the kingdom of their Father' (13:43).

The moon too plays a certain role for Matthew. He shares with the other two Synoptic Gospel writers an account of apocalyptic changes that will befall the sun, the moon and the stars (24:29), even though, in his case, the superficially 'identical' statement is given an inner enrichment through the consonance with other passages. The Transfiguration is followed, after the descent, by the healing of the possessed boy, whom the remaining nine disciples had tried in vain to help. Only Matthew has for this boy the diagnosis of *seleniazomenos* (17:15). This does not necessarily mean 'moonstruck' in the narrower sense. It means that the boy is under the one-sided influence of forces which, coming from the night-side of the soul-life, out of the dark lower strata not controlled by the ego, 'throw the sufferer now into the fire, now into the water.' These unbalanced soul forces have for Matthew the quality of the moonlike. The Christ brings to the healing the sunlike which can subdue these uncontrolled forces. This is how close 'sun' and 'moon' are here. By virtue of the confrontation between sun and moon, the sequence of these two stories, which is the same in Mark and Luke, assumes a cosmic aspect in Matthew's account. Precisely through this sequence it becomes evident that comparison to the sun in relation to the Transfiguration are more than only incidentally poetic. Once more, in another passage, Matthew speaks of *seleniazómenoi,* of 'moon-sufferers.' They are mentioned, along with other categories of patients, at the beginning of the Christ's healing work (4:24).

In this connection it should also be noted that Matthew was the only one to speak of the '*star* of Magi' (2:1–12). 'Magi' were the Persian priests. Here is a curious fact of history: When in the year 614, the Persians devastated Jerusalem, they spared the Church of Birth in Bethlehem, because the Wise Men from the Orient, on their pilgrimage to the star, were portrayed wearing Persian garb.

If one looks more deeply into the references to 'sun, moon and stars' in Matthew's gospel, then the well-known fact that *'heaven,'* or rather 'the heavens' and 'heavenly,' are favourite words of Matthew, appears in a new light. While Luke speaks of the 'kingdom of God,' Matthew always says: 'the kingdom of the heavens.' Equally, he speaks several times of the heavenly Father. It has been said, by way of explanation, that devout Jews preferred to speak of heaven rather than of God. That may also play a part. However, a special interest in the cosmic heavens and its manifestations are unmistakable. Behind the plural, 'the heavens,' stands the old perception that the supersensible world which expresses itself 'physiognomically' in astronomical phenomena, is in itself variously graded.

Another peculiarity of Matthew is that he repeats several times the formula 'heaven and earth' (5:34f; 6:10; 16:19; 18:18f;

28:18), from the Sermon on the Mount to the revelation of the Risen One on the mountain in Galilee. In his version of the Lord's Prayer Matthew preserves the contents with a cosmic ring, a Persian-Zarathustrian note, which are missing in Luke. Going beyond Luke, Matthew says in his address: Father 'in the heavens.' The third petition is missing in Luke. It is directed towards the will of the Father, which is done in heaven, but must yet be made truly effective on earth. Heaven is the realm of light where the will of the Father is done. The earth has been darkened by the forces of the Adversary and is yet to become the scene of activity for the divine will. Accordingly, the seventh petition, not found in Luke, says: 'Deliver us from the evil.' The Persian view of the world appreciated the dualist element in the world, the battle situation that exists between light and dark, the necessity to conquer the earth for the realm of light. Wherever Matthew goes beyond Luke in the Lord's Prayer, there is this particular ingredient.

Thus the *'earth,'* as being of a special kind, is also placed into cosmic context. The word *gē,* earth, can otherwise often mean simply 'land.' But it has to be meant in a 'telluric' sense, when the Christ says that the Son of Man will 'dwell in the heart of the earth' (12:40) — a truly unique formulation. The same applies when 'salt of the earth' is mentioned (5:13). In the account of the Good Friday darkness 'across the whole land,' *gē* means, first of all, the land around Jerusalem, Judea, *erez Israel.* But at the same time 'land' also stands for 'earth' here. And if, after death has occurred, 'the earth shakes,' it is still 'the earth' as special cosmic body, as 'cosmic individuality' as it were, which reacts as such to the events of Golgotha with the rending of rocks and the opening of tombs (27:51f), just as on the morning of Easter she again accompanies the Resurrection with a 'great earthquake.'

From these observations on sun, moon and stars it follows that the gospel of Matthew must be credited with a certain world-embracing cosmic interest. It also gives the description of the Transfiguration its peculiar tinge.

Moses and Elijah

The Christ was 'transformed before them.' 'Before them' shows that the event has its beginning in ordinary perception and, as it progresses towards the supersensible, the consciousness of the disciples also develops towards visionary beholding. The appearance of Moses and Elijah, both of whom no longer belong to the earthly world, quite decidedly comes within the sphere of a purely clairvoyant perception and has no beginning in the earthly visible. It is introduced by the rousing 'behold!' *And behold, there allowed himself to be seen Moses, and Elijah talking with him* (17:3). Allowed 'himself' not 'themselves' as one would expect, since two names are involved. Against all expectations the singular is used and relates therefore to Moses only, with Elijah being added somewhat superficially with an 'and.' There can be no doubt that for Matthew the stronger accent is on Moses.

Not in the selection only, but also in the arrangement of the scriptures which together make up the New Testament, especially the gospels, there is a good deal of wisdom. And Matthew, too, was allotted his rightful place. Matthew is the 'liaison man' between the Old Testament and the New. Not only is he, as the first author of the New Testament, visibly closest to the Old Testament, but he is also the one who most frequently refers back to the Old Testament. Again and again he points to prophecies being fulfilled. 'This happened so that what had been written may be fulfilled ...' It is used much more frequently by Matthew than by any of the other evangelists. To a higher degree than the other evangelists, Matthew shows a retrospective interest. Now the Old Testament, although not yet finally delineated at the time of the Christ, was seen in the duality of 'Law and Prophets,' with Moses again gravitating towards the past, while Elijah was felt to be the genius of prophecy, pointing to the future. So it accords with the nature of Matthew that he should develop, within the

Old Covenant, a stronger relationship with Moses who, proclaiming the law with paternal authority, was orientated towards the beginnings. For him Moses stands 'out front,' and not only in a superficially historical sense.

In dealing with the Luke text we said that in the spirit-radiance of the Moses figure there was present something of the 'glory of the Father,' and in that of Elijah something of the 'glory of the Holy Spirit.' In speaking of the sunlike quality of the Christ, Matthew established a special reference back to an important statement in the Old Testament. In the final chapter of the book of Malachi, the last of the books of prophets at the very end of the Old Testament, the Christ is heralded as 'the Sun of Righteousness.' Following the announcement of the angel who prepares the way, the text says: 'But to you who fear my name, the Sun of Righteousness shall arise with healing in his wings' (Mal.4:2). And immediately afterwards: 'Remember the law of Moses, my servant, which I have commanded him on Horeb ...'(4:4) and: 'Behold, I will send you Elijah, the prophet, before the coming of the great and dreadful day of the Lord' (4:5). To Moses belongs the retrospective memory, while Elijah is connected with the preview of apocalyptic catastrophies and the eschatological conclusion. This book of Malachi reads like a testament, like a summary of the Old Covenant. In the first book of the New Testament, Matthew shows the fulfillment. Christ as Sun of Righteousness become Human, standing between Moses and Elijah.

Peter

In keeping with his quick-tempered personality, Peter feels an impulse to take an active part in the event on the Transfiguration mountain. Matthew and Mark say specifically that he 'answered.' 'Peter answered and said to Jesus: Lord, it is good that we are here. If you want it, I will build three tabernacles here, one for you, one for Moses and one for Elijah' (17:4).

Luke has Peter address the Christ with *Epistata,* something like 'Master' with the connotation of a leader of an esoteric community. In Mark we find the humanly unselfconscious 'Rabbi.' As he does elsewhere, Matthew uses the most reverential address: 'Lord' — *Kyrie.* In keeping with this reverence is also the 'if you want it.' A further peculiarity is the singular: 'I will build' rather than 'we.' This shows the person of Peter to be more prominent as a special individuality.

Already in the scene at Caesarea Philippi we had occasion to notice how, in Matthew's version, more space is given to the person of Peter than Mark gives him, let alone Luke, who only records the word of confession, but is silent about the rest. The hard word 'Satan' is found also in Mark, but Matthew, in addition, makes Peter having to cope with the reproach that he gives offence to the Christ.

Peter's protest against the announced suffering and death must be seen in a wider context. On the mountain of temptation to dominate the world, the Christ, only recently incarnated into the earthly body, encounters the endeavours of the Adversary to divert him from the path of sacrifice, which means earthly failure and violent death. The Adversary wants to prevent the mystery of Golgotha. By rejecting the temptation, the Christ restates his resolution to go through with the sacrifice, a decision that was made already in the higher world before his descent and taken with him into his incarnation. He sends the Adversary away and thereby signs his own death warrant.

But the Adversary has not given up yet. After the first announcement of the Passion he makes use of Peter who, owing to his lack of spiritual wakefulness, unintentionally serves as his mouthpiece: This must not happen to you! The Christ immediately recognizes the real speaker, namely 'Satan.' He recognizes that the temptation not to tread the road to Golgotha is here again in a different guise. At this moment, Peter's reaction to the reference to the Passion is to him the 'affront' which would like to cause his downfall. Looked at from this vantage point, the words on the Transfiguration mountain spoken by Peter with less than full consciousness, as Mark and Luke stress explicitly, appear in a strange light. It is then not only a naive expression of bliss connected with the higher experience to the extent that, being in a state akin to euphoria, he completely forgets the misery prevailing down in the valley, and desires to be and to remain only 'up here.' His spiritual delight is tinged with a selfish element. It is good to be here — a Luciferic nuance is noticeable here.

Rudolf Steiner drew parallels between the Transfiguration of the Christ and the death of the Buddha and his entry into Nirvana, stressing that for the Christ the great mystery really only begins in earnest when, once more, he gathers his divine being into himself for the final descent into the Passion. The Christ is indeed quite close to the threshold of death on the mountain. He appears already to belong more to this other world that is home to him, the air of which he breathes on the mountain retreat. And once more he must confirm his resolve to embrace the sacrifice that had been decided. An indication that the descent into the valley was a sacrifice can be found in the succeeding story of the healing of the 'moonstruck' boy. Immediately after the descent, the Christ encounters anew, down in the lowlands, 'all of humanity's misery,' not only in the form of the affliction but also, and not least, in the spiritual impotence of his disciples. He utters a word then that, coming from his lips, might sound almost strange to us, a word in which something like annoyance is expressed. 'Oh, faithless and perverse generation! How long shall I be with you yet? How much longer shall I have to put up with you?' (17:17). After having breathed again the air of higher worlds, the effluvium of human souls hits him like a suffocating wave. 'How much longer?' But in an instant this moment of despair is conquered, and with renewed will he turns lovingly to earthly needs: 'Bring him to me!' — This 'how much longer' is also found in Mark and Luke but Matthew strikes a special note inasmuch as he gives more prominence to the temptation, and it is he who has the word of the Risen One at the end of his book: 'Behold! I am with you always even to the end of the world' (28:20). This answers the question: 'How much longer shall I be with you?'

The Christ does not allow the Transfiguration event to turn into a premature, light-happy, dying-away. The descent from the mountain is followed by the second announcement of the Passion (17:22), and according to Luke (9:51) this is the beginning of the road to Jerusalem. Peter, however, had 'answered' to the Transfiguration in a direction which ran contrary to the scheme of salvation, even if this time the temptation is more hidden than it was in the blunt protest at Caesarea Philippi.

The light-cloud

While Peter was still talking, *'behold, a light-cloud overshadowed them'* (17:15). Matthew introduces the phenomenon with 'behold,' the second 'behold' in his report. It is one of Matthew's well-known peculiarities that he makes frequent use of this behold, beginning with the first appearance of the angel before the dreaming Joseph (1:20), to the mighty behold of the very last sentence — 'behold, I am with you all the days.' Mostly it is a call to be aware of something supersensible approaching. The first 'behold' was aimed at the appearance of Moses and Elijah, the second at the cloud (the latter only in Matthew). He says of the cloud that it is 'lightlike' *(phōteinē)*. This gives the phenomenon an even stronger accent towards the supersensible. It is a light-cloud, similar to the 'white cloud' in the Apocalypse that carries the returning Son of Man (14:14).

The cloud-space, mediating between heaven and earth, yet still belonging to the earth, represents an area of earthly existence that has not entered the solidifying process but remained pliant. Looking at the clouds one can observe, taking place in a delicate medium, becoming and dissolving, shaping and reshaping. It is a realm of possibilities that washes around the solid earth. Gazing into the clouds could stimulate the soul and trigger clairvoyant perception. The Ascending Christ, as well as the Returning One, appears 'in the clouds' — since the Ascension the Christ is active in that part of the earth-being that is still pliant and upwardly open, offering new possibilities, and in this mode of being of his can he be beheld, if by gazing at the clouds the spiritual eye can be opened to higher perceptions. There is nothing to demythologize in the statement of the 'Return in the Clouds.' It only needs an understanding of this picture-language which lives on the border of 'real' and 'unreal,' of 'sensible' and 'supersensible.' It is still valid today.

The 'light-cloud' of Matthew is reminiscent of the auric fabric which hides as well as reveals the deity whose presence is felt at cultic worship. The Old Testament speaks of a cloud which, at the inauguration of the cult, enveloped the tabernacle, the interior of which was filled with the glory of the Lord (Exod.40:34). When the Temple of Solomon was consecrated, 'the cloud filled the house, and the priests could not attend to their ministry because of the cloud, for the glory of the Lord filled the house' (1Kings 8:10f). This light-cloud showing itself in the interior of the temple is something perceived supersensibly. At the Transfiguration the vision may have been aided by an atmospheric cloud formation such as can easily be imagined to occur around the peak of a mountain.

Out of this light-cloud the voice of God is heard. In Matthew it is preceded by his third 'behold':

And behold, a voice from the cloud saying, this is my beloved Son in whom I have revealed myself. Hear him. (17:5)

It would be easy to suspect Matthew of literary 'preference' being obviously unaware of the fact that the optical word 'behold,' used by him so frequently, does not really fit the auditory experience of the voice. Reading Matthew's account of the Jordan Baptism, one finds a similar sentence. While Mark and Luke do not have 'behold' in their account of the Baptism, Matthew uses it twice over. 'And behold, the heavens opened' (3:16). 'And behold, a voice from the heavens' (3:17). As it was at the Transfiguration, there first came an impression of light (the heavens opened) and then something is heard (the voice). Both times the 'behold.' Before charging Matthew with literary carelessness that does not stay with the image, one should try to gain an insight into these two descriptions of his relating to the Baptism and the Transfiguration respectively. First of all, there is the lightlike quality where 'behold' is organically quite appropriate. One can detect in Matthew altogether a certain enthusiasm for light and seeing when, for example, he speaks of the star of Bethlehem:

Behold, there came wise men ... we have *seen* his star
... and *behold,* the star which they *saw* in the East ...
when they *saw* the star they rejoiced with great joy ...
and entering *saw* the child ... (2:1-12).

One could imagine that for Matthew the ringing revelation of the word, belonging to a still higher spiritual region, passes through the sphere of the lightlike and is tinged by it. Thus, the heavenly voice, as it first rings out, is for him still more of a light-experience. We too speak of the light and dark of a voice, and we can express tone qualities through light qualities and vice versa.

In Matthew the word of the Transfiguration accords with the word of the Baptism, both times in the third person saying: 'He is ...' The close relationship between the two events is underlined by this parallel, just as at other times Matthew shows a tendency in his gospel to duplicate certain terminologies. But on the other hand, the event-like character of the Baptism ('you are ...') is not so clearly distinguished from the descriptive character of the Transfiguration ('this is ...').

The fear of the disciples

'Hear him! — And the disciples heard and fell on their faces and were very afraid' (17:5f). According to Mark and Luke the fear originated with the appearance of Moses and Elijah (Mark 9:6), or rather their entry into the cloud (Luke 9:34). With Matthew it is the overwhelming experience of the voice of God that throws the disciples down in fear. They were 'very' afraid. Matthew is the one who puts the greatest emphasis on this; he alone speaks of the disciples' 'falling down on their faces.' Just as he of all the evangelists could best relate to the divine Father-principle, so also to the element of divine authority to which human beings respond with awe and worship. With Matthew the Christ, too, has a share in this majestic dignity commanding reverence. The Christ-image of Matthew's gospel is of a positively iconesque solemnity. We have already noted a preference for the address 'Kyrie' which can reach right into the divine.

This gesture of worship and prostration runs through all of Matthew's gospel, from the Magi in Bethlehem who fall to their knees and worship the Child, to the disciples on the Easter mountain in Galilee.

It is usual, when speaking of such worshipful prostrations, to take into account the established theophanic narrative and the 'court-style' of oriental potentates. The petitioner who was granted an audience threw himself down in front of the great king and waited until it was indicated to him that he may rise. One must not be satisfied with the mere comparative reference to such ceremonies. Surely one must ask where the real origin lies. Falling down and being picked up is not without significance in relation to the religious archetypal mystery of life and death and resurrection. When a human being is granted a theophany, an impression of the world of the divine, then the whole inadequacy of his own being vis-a-vis the divine is brought home to him with shattering force. His whole being appears to be questionable. 'He, who sees God, dies.' The human being dies who has lived the way he has up to this moment. He dies in this encounter. But that which makes him die, also awakens him to a higher life. The human being who walks away from this experience is not the same as before. As one born anew, he has risen from death.

Therefore, one does not do justice to a scene of the disciples falling down on their faces at the Transfiguration, as described by Matthew, by pointing to theophanic style and court ceremonial, and leaving it at that. One cannot attempt to derive and 'explain' the gospels from such habits and customs. In fact, the opposite is true. The disciples experience what happens with even stronger intensity to the seer John on Patmos. He sees the elevated Christ whose 'countenance shines like the sun in his strength.' 'And when I saw him, I fell at his feet as dead. And he laid his right hand on me and said: "Fear not".' (Rev.1:17). And at the Transfiguration: *And Jesus came close and touched them and said: rise and do not be afraid!* (17:7). On other occasions, we only hear about the Christ touching people in relation to healing, or to the children he blessed. The touch was no mere symbol. Something enlivening emanated from the Christ's hand. The scene at the conclusion of the Transfiguration is unique in the Synoptic Gospels; nowhere else does the Christ 'touch' the disciples, except at the washing of feet described by John. He does for them what later on he will do for John on Patmos. He awakens them back to life from dying of the divine.

The fact that the word of comfort 'fear not' is used in many of the narratives dealing with the appearance of a supersensible being, cannot simply be dismissed with a reference to 'theophanic' or 'epiphanic' style. One should seek the truth by asking what experienced reality may be hidden behind it.

'And when they lifted up their eyes they saw no one but Jesus alone' (17:8). The lifting of eyes, at other times often an expression for being on the verge of having a vision, is explained here by what went before, namely that the disciples had fallen 'on their faces.' There is something reverential in this expression. The disciples become aware that the supersensible experience of a 'partial' mystical death has come to a conclusion with this event. The ordinary everyday consciousness has returned. Once more they see in front of them Jesus of Nazareth in familiar guise.

'Do not speak to anybody about this'

'And when they came down from the mountain, Jesus charged them and said: "Do not speak to anybody about this vision until the Son of Man is risen again from the dead".' (17:9).

The Greek text shows a minor unevenness here: when they descended 'out of' the mountain, Mark and Luke use the expected 'from' *(apo)*. Although the 'out of' is linguistically inappropriate, the text was faithfully handed down in this form. A cause to be thankful: for sometimes, in the linguistically and logically incorrect, an attempt may be hidden to express something that is difficult to put into words. Thus the 'out of' may want to express a certain nuance of the experience the disciples had, that while they were on the mountain they felt themselves to be 'inside something' that embraced them until they stepped out of it again on descending. They are not only 'down-going ones' but also, at the same time, 'out-going ones.'

The supersensible experience, now concluded, is, according to Matthew, described by the Christ as a 'vision,' something 'visually perceived'; *(hórama* in Greek, from *horaō* — seeing).

About this vision the disciples are not to speak with anyone. Luke showed the other side. The disciples themselves 'were silent.' In Matthew and Mark the silence is imposed on them as an explicit command. These two aspects do not necessarily contradict each other. They complement each other. In the no-talking command of the Christ an important principle is involved that goes beyond the text of Luke. Supersensible experiences are of a delicate nature and must be handled with care. If they are communicated, they are in danger of being 'talked to pieces' and must therefore be protected by a sheath of silence.

Here at the Transfiguration the issue was not only that the secret of the nature of the Christ Jesus should remain within the circle of twelve, as had been impressed on the disciples after Peter's confession at Caesarea Phillipi: 'Then he charged the disciples that they should tell no man that he was Jesus, the Christ' (16:20). The renewed command to keep silent in the wake of the Transfiguration, restrains the three witnesses in relation also to the rest of their fellow apostles. It does not refer to the knowledge that in Jesus lives the Son of God, this having been pronounced by Peter in the hearing of the disciples and accepted by the Christ. Now the command refers to the supersensible experience, the 'vision.' In accordance with esoteric law, proper 'follow-up treatment' is required, that is, it must be enfolded in silence. This enables it to work all the better in the souls of the disciples until, after a certain time, it reaches the maturity necessary for it to be pronounced. As the child develops in the secrecy of the womb until it is allowed to see the light of day, so also should the experience that is wrapped in silence pass through a stage of development 'until the Son of Man is raised from the dead.'

The Transfiguration now, having been absorbed into the meditative silence of the disciples, becomes itself the starting point for a future path at the end of which waits the Resurrection. Just as the first signs of an inner all-penetrating light initiate an understanding of the body's possibilities to undergo a spiritualizing process, so the Transfiguration opens up a further path at the end of which penetration by the spirit will have led to total spiritualization. But this is the crescendo that leads from Transfiguration to Resurrection. The Transfiguration beheld by the three disciples is, in the following months, expected to mature in their souls to the point where, when the time comes, it can to a certain extent facilitate some understanding of the Easter events.

The appearance of the Resurrection motive at conclusion of the Transfiguration narrative, prompts us to return once more to Bultmann's thesis mentioned at the beginning, asserting that the Transfiguration account is a 'back-dated Easter story.' Although the connection between Transfiguration and Resurrection was being felt, the very obvious difference had not been taken seriously enough, thus giving rise to an incorrect interpretation of the relationship. The 'and is already now' of the Transfiguration preceding the Easterly 'it will be,' is misunderstood. At the Damascus vision of Paul and the apocalyptic Patmos vision of John, this glory of the Risen One whose corporeality had undergone a further spiritualizing process through his Ascension, shone forth in full splendour. The Ascension is conclusion and crowning of a process through which the resurrected body has passed during the forty days — and of course it is the Ascension narrative that provides the bridge to the Second Coming in the clouds (Acts 1:11). The Second Coming is connected with becoming aware of the 'great glory' (Matt.24:30). We mentioned earlier that the words spoken by the Christ eight days before the Transfiguration anticipate the future as far ahead as 'the coming of the Son of Man in his glory.' The Transfiguration with its glorious light-revelation mirrors a far-away future which, pointing beyond the Easter Day itself, will have grown out of the Resurrection event from where it had taken its origin.

The conversation about Elijah

The admonition to keep silent is followed, during the descent, by a conversation about Elijah. The disciples have beheld him as one of the two spirit figures, and now they wonder what to think of the prophecy that Elijah would have to come before the Messiah. The Christ confirms the prophecy and shows that it has already been fulfilled. Elijah has already accomplished his precursor mission in the guise of a personality whom his contemporaries did not recognize as the transitory Elijah individuality. Here Matthew — and only Matthew — follows up with a momentous sentence: 'Then the disciples understood that he had spoken to them of John the Baptist' (17:13).

Thereby a reference is made to something that happened earlier. The Christ had once talked about the Baptist, and in this context made a statement that again we know only from Matthew: 'And if you will accept it, it is Elijah who is to come. He who has ears let him hear' (11:14). Nowhere else in the gospels is it said with such clarity: 'He is Elijah.' This statement of an instance of reincarnation is presented to the consciousness of the listeners with the addition: 'if you will accept it.' Since that time the disciples had carried the word in their souls. Now, after the Transfiguration event, the organic point in time for this 'accepting' has come. 'Then the disciples understood.'

Maybe it is not entirely accidental that this insight comes after a transformation experience. The word 'metamorphosis' was used in connection with Jesus. The metamorphosis of Rabbi Jesus into a radiant sunlike figure is the previewed reflection of ultimate perfection accomplished in the Resurrection. The Risen One realizes in his person now what will not be within reach of humanity before Judgement Day. With his wholly spiritualized body that is no longer subject to death, the Risen One puts the ultimate great metamorphosis of the human being into the present cosmic age 'already now,' as a piece of future 'inoculated' into the present impelling it towards its coming conclusion. On Easter Day the Christ attains for himself, with the giant strides of a God, what for humanity is still a faraway goal. The road to Judgement Day is a long one and reincarnations have their place on it as comparatively 'minor metamorphoses' which finally lead Christian humanity to the ultimate 'great metamorphosis' — step by step, 'From glory to glory' (2Cor.3:18). So, too, the further transformation of Elijah of the Old Testament into a man like John serving the Christ comes to stand in the light of the Transfiguration

167

metamorphosis of the Christ Jesus, and the disciples perceive it in just this light. 'Then the disciples understood.'

Again Matthew emerges as the liaison between the Old Testament and the New. Again and again we see him concerned to preserve continuity from the preceding salvation story of Israel on to the present. This continuity cannot be expressed more strongly than by showing that there is a connection by reincarnation. A leading individuality of the Old Covenant has, at the close of an age, reappeared as John the Baptist, and through his own person he binds, in a living way, the Old Testament to the New.

20. According to Mark

Inspiration

We began with the Transfiguration as presented in the third gospel because Luke, by his more intimate psychological description, makes more accessible a kind of experience which, initially, is foreign to present-day consciousness. In sharp contrast stands the quite different way of Matthew. The characteristics of these two evangelists become clearly perceptible in their divergence in the Transfiguration narrative in particular.

On reading the Transfiguration of Mark one may well first gain the impression that it is almost identical with Matthew's account, though certain important features of the latter are omitted, and also that it hardly adds anything of note that is not yet known from the gospels of Matthew and Luke. A widely held theological opinion has it that Mark's gospel was written first and was already known to Matthew and Luke who worked it into their accounts. This view, however plausible it may appear at first glance, has also had its opponents and, we believe, with justification. In detail, a good many observations do not fit this hypothesis. Confronted with the actual text, one would do well to consider that various streams of oral history flowed into the gospels with some features being identical, although the streams were independent of one another. The power of true memory was incomparably stronger in former times than it is now.

The fact that there is a connection to oral traditions is no contradiction to the gospels being truly inspired. In an era where concrete perceptions of the supersensible had ceased to exist, a completely unrealistic, mechanistic inspiration doctrine was developed that was bound to arouse opposition, and that led eventually to the baby being thrown out with the bath water, nobody wanting to hear anymore of 'inspiration.' Now the gospels were treated as quite ordinary literature. To this rigid inspiration doctrine it made no difference whether Mark, as a pupil of Peter's, may still hear his tutor's narrating voice, or not, it being thought irrelevant to inspiration. A living interpretation of inspiration will include such references. Just as the fact that inspiration makes use of available words and linguistic tools is no argument against it, so too it is feasible that it can incorporate, organically, what has been spoken into more comprehensive word structures.

To begin with, let us have Mark's text in front of us:

And he said to them: 'Amen, I tell you there are some standing here who will not taste death before they have seen the kingdom of God coming in force *[dynamis].'* After six days Jesus takes with him Peter and James and John and 'carries' them up a high mountain alone by themselves. And he was transfigured before them. And his raiment became glistening, exceedingly white as snow, as no fuller on earth can make them white. And there appeared to them Elijah with Moses and they were talking with Jesus. And Peter answered and said to Jesus: 'Master, it is good for us to be here and let us build three tabernacles: one for you, one for Moses and one for Elijah,' because he did not know what he said for they were sore afraid; and there came about a cloud that overshadowed them and a voice happened out of the cloud: 'This is my beloved Son. Hear him!' And suddenly, when they had looked about them, they saw no man any more save Jesus alone with them. And as they came down from the mountain he charged them that they should tell no man what they had seen till the Son of Man were risen from the dead. And they kept this saying with themselves, questioning one with another what the rising from the dead should mean. And they asked him saying: 'Why say the scribes that Elijah must first come ...' (9:1–11).

The fact that we first turned our attention to the presentation by Luke and Matthew resulted in us having already dealt with individual features of the report. However, a closer look at Mark's text will reveal some peculiarities in spite of the apparent similarities, especially with Matthew.

Unearthly light

Mark desists from commenting on the countenance of the Transfigured One. Like Matthew he uses the word *metemorphōthē* — 'he was transformed' — and then turns his attention to the garments. 'And his raiment became glistening, exceedingly white as snow, as no fuller on earth can make them white' (9:3). To the light-describing words of the other evangelists he also adds *stilbō* (glistening), a word that can also describe the sparkle of heavenly bodies. It appears only here in the New Testament.

'White' *(leukos)* is common to all three Synoptic Gospel writers. Mark underlines it with 'exceedingly.' Like Matthew he also speaks of 'snow' — he too makes use of the geographical reference to the region around Caesarea Philippi, thereby including Hermon. But Mark adds his own comparison for the special quality of this snowy light: the fuller who is not able to make anything so exceedingly white, no fuller 'on earth.'

This comparison was sometimes felt to be somewhat childish. E. Lohmeyer, to whom we are otherwise indebted for some sensitive observations, speaks of the 'village-horizon' of such a picture. At the same time, the term 'on earth' is of great importance here. It plays a major role in all three Synoptic Gospels.

'On earth' — this is how Matthew refers to that region of the world that has its opposite in the 'uranic' regions of the heavens. In the heavens the will of God is done, while the earth is fought over and has yet to be regained for the light. Through the Christ's incarnation, heaven and earth enter a new reciprocal relationship. The 'as in the heavens, so also on earth' is also subject to reversal. Christian earth-impulses may also weave into the heavenly worlds, 'as on earth so also in the heavens' (Matt.16:19; 18:18; 18:19). The Risen One holds both worlds in his hand, he has authority 'in heaven and on earth' (28:18).

'On earth' — in Mark's gospel, too, this word that seems to appear so casually in the Transfiguration narrative is not unique. Earlier there was the healing of the man suffering from palsy when the Christ tells the scribes that the Son of Man has authority to forgive sins 'on earth' (2:10; also Matt.9:6; Luke 5:24). For the 'pre-Christian' perception, authority for forgiving sins could only be found in a world that lay beyond anything human, that was purely heavenly. Now this authority became effective at the divine-human level through the Christ Jesus in human form — 'on earth.' The Christ Jesus has brought down into the earthly human world what previously had been heavenly only. With him something quite new comes towards the earth and humanity. This new element is felt by Mark when, with his 'fuller' comparison, he tries to say that with the Christ a light enters the earthly world that is absolutely 'not of this earth.' The white garment has at all times had an obvious pictorial meaning. The washing of a soiled garment and the inner cleansing of the soul's tarnished sheath became interchangeable in the perception of people of old, when inwardness and outwardness were not yet divided so abstractly. The white garment was the goal of all cleansing endeavour of the old religions, to which all who strove came closer to a greater or lesser degree. But only the Christ Jesus makes recognizable what is meant by this ideal, what the 'white garment' is in truth. Beyond all that which earthly 'whitening'-endeavours can achieve, the Christ brings down to earth his light which has the purity of snow.

It is a light 'not of this earth' and yet, at the same time, 'for' this earth. It is, of course, not so that it appears from outside once only, illuminating an outstanding figure, only to allow earthbound humanity to sink back into darkness more hopeless than ever. It is no heavenly mirage but the announcement that this heavenly substance is about to communicate with earthly humanity. However, the only way to reach human beings is through death and resurrection of the Christ who, through his suffering a human death, has so transformed his heavenly being that it becomes accessible to humans, that it becomes communicable.

The Transfiguration is very soon followed by the second announcement of the Passion, just as it was preceded by the first one at Caesarea Philippi. This second announcement of the Passion has a unique form. It alone contains the motif of the 'Son of Man who shall be delivered into the hands of men' (Mark 9:31; Matt.17:22; Luke 9:44). In fact, Luke omits any other prediction of the Passion or Resurrection, leaving only this one — 'the Son of Man delivered into the hands of men.' It is most certainly a prediction of the Passion. The One, who is without sin, wearer of snow-white garments spun of light, will be delivered into the killing hands of the sinners. But at the same time, behind this strange formula — 'the Son of Man delivered into the hands of men' — there appears, as from afar, another interpretation of meaning, in accordance with the 'paradox' of the mystery of Golgotha, which hints at a positive aspect that can only come into being at the cost of the Passion. The Apocalypse of John sees Christened human beings of the future who have washed and 'whitened' their garments in the blood of the Lamb (7:14). The same verb *leukainō* ('whiten') is used as in the Transfiguration text of Mark.

Elijah and Moses

With Matthew we noticed that for him Moses is apparently more important than Elijah. 'And behold, there showed himself Moses and Elijah' (17:3), Not showed 'themselves' but 'himself' in the singular! It is exactly the opposite in Mark: *'there showed himself Elijah with Moses'* (9:4). Here too the singular that takes note of only one of the spirit figures. But with Mark it is not Moses, but Elijah.

Mark shows in his whole gospel that he is not interested in the past to the same degree as Matthew. He does not present a genealogical tree, be it the one according to Matthew that leads back to Israel's beginnings, or the one according to Luke that reaches to the beginnings of humanity in Adam. He does not relate childhood stories. He begins with the point in time of the Baptism in the Jordan, and puts in front of his book the absolute word *archē,* 'beginning.' It is not the beginning of the world that is meant, nor the beginning of Israel, or even the beginning of the life of Jesus, but what is done to the adult Jesus through John the Baptist. This is for Mark *the* new beginning, once more in the grand manner a beginning of creation. What had been before this impact remains unmentioned.

Mark is first and foremost concerned with a happening that begins with the Jordan Baptism and strives forcefully in a series of deed-inspired events towards the mystery of death and resurrection. The bare essentials having been said about John the Baptist, verse 9 of the first chapter already confronts us with the Jordan Baptism. In connection with it, the word *euthys,* 'immediately,' enters the narrative for the first time, a word that is so typical of Mark and his impetuous will-orientated character, appearing as it does no less than 41 times in his gospel. 'And immediately, coming out of the water, he saw the heavens rent open ...' (1:10). 'And immediately the Spirit drives him out into the wilderness' (1:12).

This emphasis on will can be attributed to the fact that Mark brings so much less teaching content than the other evangelists. For him the teacher makes way for the doer. So it is that Elijah with his spiritual fire-nature that drives him forward towards decisions and the future is closer to him than Moses. Certainly, Moses too was in the highest sense a 'doer.' But in the consciousness of his people he was first and foremost the great teacher, 'learned in all the wisdom of Egypt' (Acts 7:22). Matthew has the word of the *kathedra,* the chair of Moses (23:2). There could be no question of a 'chair of Elijah.' Elijah, 'the burning and shining lamp' (John 5:35), is all blazing will. He has to prepare what is in the future and is always a 'coming one.' Fiery, future-orientated will is also Mark's element. For him it is important that the kingdom of God come 'with power' (9:1). He alone describes the Easter angel as a 'young man' (16:5). Easter is for him the youth-restoring beginning of the world.

Out of this upward and forward striving impulse Mark, in the Transfiguration narrative, puts Elijah before Moses.

The share of the three disciples

An apparently unimportant aspect at the beginning of the Transfiguration narrative can attract attention. As in Matthew, the Christ 'takes' the three chosen disciples 'unto himself' and 'carries them up' the mountain, Matthew adding *kat'idian,* 'apart' (17:1). We have already mentioned that in *idios* lies the reference to the 'essence' and the 'essential,' to a value that is of significance to the human being as individual ego-being. Mark also has this *kat'idian* but he adds *monous* (9:2), the plural of *monos* (in the accusative mode). This word has a certain dignity-denoting quality. Any other time it is reserved only for the Christ himself. *Monos* — the unique one, the one who carries the secret of the 'one'-ness of the eternal 'I' within himself.

One could be excused for thinking that the fact of the Christ-event made its influence felt across time, when in the third post-Christian century the mystic Plotinus, regarding himself as a non-Christian, finds the formulation: 'the unique only one seeking refuge with the unique only one' (concluding words of the *Enneads*). The 'one'-ness principle in the human being tends towards the great 'one'-ness principle of the world. Only in that which is Christian could these words find total fulfillment, the human ego taking refuge with the great sheltering EGO, protector from egotism, that has appeared in the Christ. 'You in me.'

With his formulation, then, Mark gives the disciples, too, their share of being *monos*. It should not be necessary to point out once more that he also wanted to establish that only these three disciples were taken up the mountain and no one else. But beyond that, it cannot be ignored that in the gospels the word *monos* is apportioned to the disciples only here.

The overshadowing

We read of the overshadowing cloud in all three Synoptic Gospels. It is an almost undetectable peculiarity of Mark that he does not construct 'overshadowing' with the expected accusative, as do both the other reporters, but with the dative. He does not say, in effect, the cloud cast a shadow 'across' them, but it cast a shadow 'to' them (9:7).

Luke also constructs overshadowing with the dative once, although not in connection with the Transfiguration but with the angel's message to Mary: 'The Holy Spirit will come upon you and the power of the Highest will cast a shadow "to" you' (1:35). No natural phenomenon is meant here, no external effect of which the human being is a mere 'object.' The dative does not show up the object-character as onesidedly radical as does the accusative. Mary, for her part, must put herself at the disposal of the Holy Spirit — 'behold, I am the handmaiden

of the Lord. It shall be done to me as you say.' In this 'it shall
be done to me' she opens herself to the heavenly influence. A
little of this nuance lies in Mark's formulation, albeit not as
expressly conscious as in Mary's Annunciation. The disciples
are not merely passive objects like earthly things on which a
shadow falls. They carry something in themselves that meets
halfway the event that is coming 'to' them and is intended to
happen 'to' them.

The question of rising from the dead

Mark brings the Christ's command not to talk about their
experience in the same way as Matthew, except that he does
not speak of a 'vision,' and that instead of 'being raised from
the dead' he says 'rising from the dead' — 'until the Son of
Man has risen from the dead' (9:9). The different nuances in
the two words are distinctly discernible in the saying Paul
quotes in his Letter to the Ephesians (5:14): 'Awake, you who
sleepeth! And arise from the dead!' Waking is the precondition. It is, of course, a well-known fact that a human being can
stand erect only when conscious. The Easter message delivered
by the angel — also according to Mark — says: 'He has been
raised from the dead.' Paul uses the same expression in his
First Letter to the Corinthians (15:4). But for the rest it should
be said that *anastēnai* is a particularly important word for
Mark. It is in keeping again with his will-powered drive.
'Rising from the dead' — in Greek also 'rising' in a wider
sense — gives a strong indication that the one who has been
raised adds his own co-operating force.

Comparing the three Passion-announcements as formulated
by the three Synoptic Gospel writers, one can observe that
Matthew uses 'be raised' on all three occasions (16:21; 17:23;
20:19), Luke once each 'be raised' (9:22) and 'rise' (18:33),
the Easter motif being omitted by Luke from the second
announcement (9:44). Mark has *anastēnai* in all three instances

(8:31; 9:31; 10:34). In close proximity to these announcements, with the thrice-repeated 'rising from the dead,' appears prominently, on conclusion of Mark's Transfiguration narrative, the Resurrection motif. What follows the word '... until the Son of Man is risen from the dead,' belongs to the passages that are peculiar to Mark. This 'speciality' of his may be inconsiderable quantitatively, but qualitatively it weighs heavily. Mark — and he alone — relates how the Christ's word of the 'Son of Man rising from the dead' strikes a chord in the disciples. *And they took hold of the word* (9:10). One could also translate it with 'they seized the word,' 'they held fast to it.' The Greek *krateō* is a word conveying will-power. Stronger than in Matthew or Luke, the activity on the part of the disciples finds expression here.

This active attitude is further apparent in the fact that the disciples, in whom the resurrection-word had sparked the desire to make it the subject of a communal effort towards knowing perception, *question one another what the rising from the dead should mean* (9:10).

It is strange that immediately afterwards they address the question concerning Elijah to the Christ. 'And they asked him and said: why do the scribes say that Elijah must come first' (9:11). They turn to the Christ with this question, one could say without any inhibitions. They do not do so with the much weightier question 'what is this: the rising from the dead' ... It is as if something was holding them back from asking the Christ, whom they had just seen transfigured, about this mystery with which he was so closely involved. So they remain among themselves with their question and together they seek to find an answer. The word 'seek together' *(syn-zētéō)* is known to us from the Emmaus story: Luke describes how the two wanderers wrestle with the riddle of the death on the cross (24:15): 'And it happened that they talked and "sought together" ...'

It is this consonance with the other passages, which are all Mark's 'speciality,' that gives weight to the statement that the

178

disciples, having taken hold with spiritual energy of the word 'rising from the dead,' now seek to comprehend through the joint endeavour of their 'selves.'

It could be argued that nothing was ever said about the disciples having taken up the Resurrection motif following any of the three Passion announcements which all conclude with the *anastēnai* and that, quite to the contrary, their total incomprehension had to be noted. From a purely logical point of view there seems to be a contradiction. But the soul-life has a logic of a special kind. It is true that the disciples have already 'with a jolt' made the transition to everyday consciousness on conclusion of the series of supersensible events. But this transition which, in principle, has been accomplished may also include the possibility that even within 'normal consciousness' a great variety of things can happen. The allusion to the Resurrection that fired the interest of the disciples did not occur until after they had begun descending the mountain. 'And while they descended from the mountain' (9:9). The descent had not yet been completed. It is still in progress. We remember the strange expression Matthew uses: while they were descending 'out of' the mountain (17:9). Precisely in its strangeness it suggests a getting 'out of' a special kind of world in which one has previously stood. An example: One wakes up in the morning, the transition to day-consciousness has already been completed, nevertheless one lingers spiritually a little while longer in this strange world of the dream just dreamt, from which one emerges only gradually. In the same way, the disciples are spiritually still 'in' the mountain experience, they are still under its spell. They have not yet arrived back 'in the valley' where they revert again to being people who may occasionally forget what once they knew. While the descent lasts, the condition of the disciples' consciousness was still 'unstable,' as it were, and during this state of transition they are still transported beyond themselves. As witnessed by the fact that, according to Matthew, they were able to grasp that Elijah has returned in the person of John the

Baptist — 'and they understood ...' (17:13). And in the ebbing away of their mountain-entrancement the word 'rising from the dead' shines powerfully into their souls.

Once more Mark uses the word *anastēnai,* namely in the story of the healing of the possessed boy down in the valley that immediately follows this passage. In this pericope Mark's literary individuality comes strongly to the fore. His dramatic narrative gives a wealth of lively detail, his account being twice as long as that of Matthew or Luke. According to Mark the people who gathered around the boy in the valley were 'shocked [amazed] when they saw him' (9:15). Being shocked or beside oneself is mentioned on other occasions only in connection with somebody witnessing an extraordinary deed of the Christ. Here, the deed has not yet been done. It is the mere sight of him who has just descended from the mountain. It seems the crowd must have perceived in the countenance of the Christ something like majesty reflected from the Transfiguration.

In the narrative of the healing of the boy that now follows, Mark has once more woven into it the great motif of death and resurrection. Matthew says: 'And the boy was healed from this hour on' (Matt.17:18). Luke has: 'And he healed the boy and gave him to his father' (Luke 9:42), emotionally human, just as the Christ 'gave the youth of Nain back to his mother' (Luke 7:15). Mark, on the other hand, dwells in detail on the process of healing. With a loud cry the daemon leaves the boy, but in departing he once more shakes him with terrible convulsions so that the boy 'became like one dead *[nekros],* the crowd saying: he has died. But Jesus took him by the hand and raised him up and he rose *[anestē]'* (9:26f). The words of the great mystery, here they are all gathered together: dead — died — raise *(egeirein)* — rise *(anastēnai).* The Greek *anastēnai* means 'rise' as well as 'rise from the dead.' The crowning 'and he rose' is *anéstē.* Of course, in the case of the boy it is not a 'rising from the dead' in the true sense, but his lying ill like one dead, and his rising through the Christ's uplifting impact, acquires a pictorial significance that can in no way be misunderstood. The event, notwithstanding its quite concrete reality, becomes transparent for still greater things to come.

We are well aware of the fact that the word *anastēnai* appears several times in the gospels without there necessarily being such transparency that relates so strongly to the Resurrection as such. Occasionally it can just mean 'arising' or 'setting out.' But the identity of the term does have its effect. The reflection of the Resurrection may be noticeable to a greater or lesser extent. It cannot be overlooked when Mark (5:42) and also Luke (8:55) say of the daughter of Jairus: *anéstē*. Not can it be overlooked when Mark weaves, in the vicinity of the Transfiguration event, this *anéstē* of the healed boy (9:27) into the tight succession of resurrection words (8:31; 9:9; 9:10; 9:31), all of which relate to the Great Mystery in the full meaning. Once again one is confronted by the phenomenon of consonance.

The special quality of Mark's report

If at first it appears that in Mark's report only very little can be found on the Transfiguration that is peculiar to Mark in the sense of a 'speciality,' closer inspection has shown that this 'speciality' does indeed exist; not so much as something distributed evenly throughout, but as an all the more impressive will-powered accent — a 'resurrection accent.'

In addition there is something else. The characteristic aspect of a gospel, the specific and the unique, cannot be clearly discerned while the eye is directed towards individual content-related items. To compare the Synoptic Gospel writers with one another only 'horizontally' would seem to be the obvious thing to do. It will reveal where the 'parallels' are, where each evangelist has his empty spaces, and where his 'speciality.' This 'horizontal' comparison of the three adjoining texts is undoubtedly justified, but one has to be aware of the danger of a certain atomizing, and of the fact that one can easily lose sight of the individual gospel as a literary whole. To complement the *horizontal* comparison, *vertical* reading must be cultivated, allowing each gospel to stand by itself, *kat'idian monon,* to have its effect as a whole without the distraction of sideways glances to its Synoptic neighbours. Then it becomes clear that the individual and the specific of an evangelist are found by no means only in his 'speciality.' One and the same event, described in like manner by all three Synoptic Gospel writers, assumes a different place value, depending on its position within that particular whole and, depending on possible 'consonance,' a specific tone colour.

As mentioned earlier, Mark, for ever driven by his will to forge ahead, confines himself in the main to describe the deeds of the Christ. With him it is not so much his 'special property' that is characteristic, but rather his 'special vacuum' — what he does not say in order that he can hurry towards the Resurrection. As a consequence, the relatively few contents of his choice assume a heightened importance of their own since there is now an empty space around them, as it were, and they now close ranks and together form the whole. The Jordan Baptism as the Great Beginning shows up in quite a different light when allowed to open the chapter without childhood or Baptist stories. It stands out more prominently as the corner-stone of the true events surrounding the Christ Jesus, balancing the other corner-stone of his death and Resurrection. And between the two the Transfiguration has its place.

Mark places it in the *centre* of his gospel. It actually is the exact centre. The number of chapters (the arrangement of the chapters dates back to the thirteenth century) obscure this as the chapters are of very different lengths. If, in order to visualize for a moment the volume of the text as such, one were to take the number of pages in Nestle's edition as measuring unit, then Mark takes up 54 pages. Without the appendix (16:9–20), an obvious addition (even though it may be written 'in the spirit' of Mark) there are 52½ pages. The Transfiguration narrative begins on page 26. Contemplation of Luke's and Matthew's texts has already shown that by its subject matter it refers back to the Jordan Baptism (the heavenly voice) as well as forward to the Resurrection. But in Mark's text this median and mediating position becomes even more markedly obvious by the Transfiguration being placed exactly in the centre of the whole, between the Jordan Baptism at the beginning and the Resurrection at the end. This centre is not intended to be a chronologically biographical one; purely externally, more time elapsed between the Jordan Baptism and the Transfiguration than between the Transfiguration and Golgotha. But measured by the inner value of the event rather than according to the exterior calendar, the Transfiguration stands in the centre.

To regard the Transfiguration as 'pre-dated,' in other words as 'Easter legend' put into the narrative without any justification, is to misunderstand the strange significance of the Transfiguration in its role as connecting link. It is in the right position.

21. Conclusion

Looking at the Gospel of John

'And we beheld his glory, the glory of the only begotten of the Father full of grace and truth' (John 1:14). Judging from this passage of John's prologue one would expect the Transfiguration story to play a significant role in the narrative of the fourth gospel. The words quoted — 'we beheld his glory' — almost sound like a personal echo confirming Luke's sentence 'they beheld his glory' (9:32). But reading on, one searches John's gospel in vain for the Transfiguration story.

John's account describes the Feeding of the Five Thousand as having taken place at the time of the Passover, making it the beginning of the last year before Golgotha. Then he jumps immediately from spring to autumn and gives a description of events connected with the autumnal Feast of Tabernacles (7:1–10:21). In between lies a span of six months. To this period of time, ignored by John, belongs the Transfiguration on the Mountain. Tradition gives as its date the 6th of August. But when John takes up his narrative again at the beginning of chapter 7, it is with the Feast of Tabernacles. Nevertheless, there is in John's text the suggestion of an echo of the Transfiguration that had gone before. The Christ, whose countenance shone like the sun, now says at the conclusion of the Feast of Tabernacles: 'I am the light of the world' (8:12). We also come across the word 'glory.'

As the Transfiguration theme is further developed by John, the question why exactly the Transfiguration narrative as such was omitted becomes even more pressing. May the author be permitted to quote a passage from Chapter 23 on the agape of the Father (see page 198) in relation to the Jordan Baptism, also omitted by John.

> The absence of just such events which one would have thought were particularly close to the heart of the fourth evangelist is altogether surprising. 'Missing' is not only the Baptism but also the Transfiguration, the Last Supper and the Ascension. On closer inspection, however, one may discern that the events missed are still contained in the gospel in some way, albeit in a finer, more 'atmospheric' form, as it were. It seems that the 'corporeality' of a concrete event-related narrative has been sacrificed, liberating in its place something of the inner essence of the event in question, permeating the text like a fragrance.

This applies particularly to the Transfiguration. What the Synoptic Gospel writers have enclosed and contained in a relatively narrow frame of narrative pericope, John has detached from the specific event, allowing it to become an element that pervades his whole gospel. What the Synoptic Gospel writers describe was an episode, a bright moment in the life of the disciples' consciousness. 'They were heavy with sleep, and awakening they beheld his glory' (Luke 9:32). Some moments later, darkening consciousness again fills the souls of the disciples; only deep down does that which they had seen continue to work towards the moment when the Son of Man would rise from the dead.

Something very special attaches to the fourth evangelist. His writings are the life-testimony of one who has been awakened and who, in describing the destiny of Lazarus, speaks of his own Christ-inspired death and resurrection experience. He is the disciple whom the Lord loves, to whom the Lord can reveal himself in a very special way. As one who has been awakened in the spirit, he has discarded the 'heaviness of sleep.' He was privileged to perceive the secret of the nature of the Christ Jesus, not only in a few sudden flashes of inner illumination, but in quiet contemplation. As far as John is concerned, the light of the Transfiguration spreads throughout the entire work of the Christ Jesus. He has come down to earth relinquishing the full brilliance of glory he has shared with the Father in eternity before the world began (17:5). Nevertheless, he brings something of the original shining magnificence into the earthly incarnation of Jesus. When, after the Jordan-Baptism, he worked his first miracle at Cana, 'he revealed his glory' (2:11). However, its full splendour can only come into being through the deed of Golgotha. At the time of the Feast of Tabernacles 'Jesus was not yet glorified,' according to John (7:39). Even on Palm Sunday the 'not yet' is still valid; here the evangelist makes the comment that, at the time, the disciples did not grasp the secret behind the entry into Jerusalem and understood only later, remembering ' when Jesus was glorified' (12:16). This *true* transfiguration can only be accomplished through the Mystery of Golgotha and its continuing effect. The Christ is again granted the glory of archetypal light that was his before the world began (17:5,24); in renewed form it arises out of the accomplished deed. We are already close in time to this 'true' transfiguration when, at the grave of Lazarus, the Christ speaks of the glorification of the Son of God (11:4), and again at the beginning of the Holy Week when, at the encounter with certain Greeks, he speaks of the glorification of the Son of Man whose hour has now come (12:23, see 17:1).

The Son's original glory is with the Father before anything else exists. Nearing incarnation during cosmic and historic ages he already had the glory which Isaiah beheld on the Pre-existing One (12:41). He manifested his glory at the beginning of his earthly work at Cana (2:11) and also on the occasion of the last of the Johannine miracles at the grave of Lazarus (11:40). And yet, prior to Golgotha he is 'not yet glorified.' In Luke, who is closest to John, and not only by virtue of the arrangement of the four gospels, we notice something similar. With him, too, the real glory is only realized through the Mystery of Golgotha. 'Did not the Christ have to suffer these things to enter into his glory' (24:26). But even earlier than that, on the Mountain of Transfiguration, the disciples saw 'his glory' (9:32). And earlier still, at Bethlehem in the Holy Night, the shepherds see the 'glory of the Kyrios, the Lord, shining round about them' (2:9), a glory that does not yet live in the body of Jesus as it does later at the Transfiguration, but still floats above the child coming from pre-existence and only now striving towards earthly destinies.

His eyes on the true Transfiguration which comes to realization only through Golgotha, the fourth evangelist can pronounce that which was granted to him as Christ-experience and Christ-knowledge, with the words: 'We saw his glory, the glory of the only begotten of the Father full of grace and truth.'

In Conclusion

Günther Bornkamm says in his book *Jesus of Nazareth* that gospel narratives like the Jordan Baptism or the Temptation in which the supersensible plays a part 'are not historical reports but descriptions, in the form of instructive narratives, of the work and nature of Jesus. This is not to deny that tradition refers to scenes from Baptism to Crucifixion and Ascension, the historical veracity of which does by no means have to be questioned. However, the possibility of detecting an historical core in these stories varies from case to case but is usually small, and each such attempt results as a rule in the loss of that which the text really wants to convey. Anybody can verify this by looking at, say, the story of the Transfiguration of Jesus which really only begins to speak to us when we no longer ask what actually happened from an historical point of view.'

We hope to have shown that regarding the Transfiguration story such a sacrifice is not called for. It is just that the concept of 'historical happening' must be clarified. The fact that mention is made of supersensible factors having had a part in a certain event does not entitle anyone to deny its historical reality. Rather it is possible that an event in which specific spiritual beings are involved may, for that very reason, become part of the fabric of occurrences known as 'history,' with enhanced significance and range of consequences. Christianity is precisely about such dynamic facts. The Christ becoming human in Jesus of Nazareth is not primarily a demonstration of timelessly valid truth which exists in any case; rather, it shows that something is *done,* something that, reaching into the future, triggers further and more distant work.

Surely it is also worth noting that the Second Letter of Peter (1:16) claims actuality in particular for the Transfiguration, in marked contrast to 'cunningly devised fables.' *Sesophismenoi mythoi* are probably myths allegorized by the awakening intellect. The events surrounding the Christ Jesus have the meaningful content in common with the myths, but they have the advantage of actuality over the latter.

We also hope to have shown that this particular way of looking at things does not result 'in the loss of that which the text really wants to convey.' In conclusion let it be said that we are convinced that a narrative like the Transfiguration story demands to be viewed in the light of 'expert knowledge' which includes the supersensible — and that only then will be revealed 'what the text wants to convey.' Only then will it really begin to speak to us.

Agape —
Divine Love in
the Fourth Gospel

22. Overview

John's Gospel is especially concerned with the Word. That is obvious not only from the Prologue, which speaks about the deepest dimensions of the Word, but also in the minute way in which the Gospel deals with its vocabulary.

Recent theology has often spoken of the 'monotony' of John's language. The general impression was that the Fourth Gospel liked to return continually to a limited number of basic concepts. The reader repeatedly confronts certain words and phrases, which are extremely significant but tend to become monotonous through constant repetition.

This impression of monotony is totally reversed when the reader realizes that such specific Johannine words and phrases are managed within the whole according to a wise economy. It appears as if the ordering within the whole and the weaving into meaningful contexts were controlled from a mysterious spiritual centre that surveys all the relationships. We need not determine here to what extent this results from the conscious intention of the author, from inspiration, or from both. Initially it is necessary only to notice the fact. Because of the economy we mentioned, each word can be given a multitude of nuances. In various passages the single word stands for this multitude and thus is able to express more than it could in isolation. Thus what first appeared as an absence of richness in colour and perspective in John's Gospel is more than compensated for.

The following will attempt to demonstrate this assertion, using the word 'agape' as an example. The word 'agape,' love, certainly belongs among the most important in John's vocabulary. A closer look at the use of this word in the course of the Gospel will give an insight into what we referred to as this Gospel's special way of dealing with the word.

Before going into details we should have a general orientation about the passages within the Fourth Gospel in which the word *agapē* or the verb *agapan* — to love with agape — are used.

It appears neither in the Prologue, nor in the first chapter (John the Baptist, the first disciples), nor in the second chapter (marriage at Cana and cleansing of the Temple).

It first appears in the conversation with Nicodemus: 'God loved the world so much' (3:16), and at the end of the conversation: 'Men have shown they prefer darkness ...' (3:19). This negative use of the word also appears at 5:42 and 8:42, which likewise point out the absence of true agape among men.

The passage 10:40-42, which reflects again on Jesus, beginning with John the Baptist, can be regarded as a division in the Gospel. If we take the first ten chapters as the first half of the Gospel, then the word 'agape' is spoken within that half only two more times in its positive, divine meaning after the conversation with Nicodemus: the Baptist's speech in which he surrenders his legacy to Christ, 'the Father loves the Son' (3:35), and at the conclusion of Christ's parable about the good shepherd, 'the Father loves me' (10:17).

In all these chapters, whose contents include the talk with the Samaritan woman, the healing of the boy, the healing of the paralytic, the feeding of the multitude and the walking on the waters, the speech about the bread of life, the controversy at the Feast of Tabernacles in Jerusalem, the healing of the blind man, the speech about the good shepherd, and the words about the Feast of the Dedication in winter — in all these chapters there are only three places in which agape is used, and in all three cases it is said about God the Father. The entire section of the first ten chapters recognizes no other bearer of agape than the Father.

A new concept appears in the chapter about Lazarus (John 11). For the first time agape is given another bearer: Christ (11:5). At the beginning of the chapter about the washing of the feet this motif of Christ's love for his own is resumed more forcefully, and in the Farewell Discourses it is as if the isolated gongs of the bell have turned into a powerful pealing. With the preceding occasional use of the word as a background, it is all the more impressive to encounter it repeatedly now. It appears seven times in Chapter 13, ten times in Chapter 14, nine times in Chapter 15, and five times in Chapter 17. In comparison to the preceding chapters that is extraordinary. Both Christ and the Father appear as bearers of agape in the Farewell Discourses; we even notice the transition to a third subject: the disciples, although in this connection it is used only as a commandment, a commission, and a future goal. But we can get an impression of the full pealing from this trio: Father-Son-disciples.

The word nearly disappears during the recounting of the Passion. In the conversation of the risen Christ with Peter by the lake, it is spoken a final time in Christ's question to Peter: 'Do you love me?' and in the evangelist's expression for the disciple, 'whom the Lord loved.'

Two observations arise at first, and we simply want to point to them as phenomena:

1. There is a difference between the first and second halves of the Gospel, that is, before and after the raising of Lazarus.

2. As bearers of agape there appear in succession Father, Son, disciples.

This alone makes it obvious that the word 'agape' is not used in John's Gospel with indiscriminate monotony.

In treating the various passages we will follow the order that is followed in the Gospel: first, the agape of the Father; secondly, the agape of the Christ; and thirdly, the agape of the disciples.

23. The agape of the Father

In the first survey we were concerned only with the bearer of agape, its subject. Another division arises when we consider the object of love. Once again we will follow the sequence observed in the Gospel: the first use of agape, in Chapter 3, speaks of the Father's love for the world.

1. The agape of the Father for the world

'God loved the world so much ...' This is probably the most sublime revelation during the conversation with Nicodemus at night. Christ had told him that no one can ascend to heaven who has not descended from heaven. What he said to Nicodemus about God's decision to redeem man is derived from an interior ascension to heaven, an elevation to the highest mysteries of the Fathers. Golgotha is predicted first in the symbolic parable of the serpent lifted up by Moses and then totally from within as if right from God's heart.

The Synoptic Gospels report that at the moment of Christ's death on the cross, the curtain of the Temple was torn. The Holy of Holies was no longer hidden from man. These words of John's Gospel in the conversation with Nicodemus can make a similar impression. During this unique hour of revelation in the night, what happens here, in truth, is symbolized by the torn curtain on Good Friday, when the Holy of Holies was revealed.

> God loved the world so much that he gave his only
> Son, so that everyone who believes in him may not be
> lost but may have eternal life (3:16).

There is no other passage in which John makes the 'world'

the object of God's love. No one else is said to have 'loved' the world except God the Father.

A good way to envisage the uniqueness of this passage is to realize that, for John, 'love of the world' is reserved for the Father.

John's Gospel gives us a sensitivity for the incomparable sublimity of the Father. The Logos creates the world (1:3) while the Father remains hidden; he is more like the silence, the nocturnal ground, out of which the Word emerges. On the other hand, since the enlightening Word is the true proclaimer and worthy 'exegete' (1:18) of the Father, his darkness is caused by the blinding unapproachable light that first becomes perceptible and accessible to man's eyes in the Son. His darkness is an excess of light and his silence an excess of sound. He is beyond our comprehension and is reached only in his Son.

On the one side it is true: 'No one has ever seen God.' But on the other side, we have: 'He who sees me sees the Father.'

He conveys himself totally in the Son, and yet the Son says, 'The Father is greater than I.'

It may be part of this 'being greater' that the Father alone is said to love the world.

'World' *(kosmos)* in the New Testament does not mean quite the same as what we call cosmic or cosmos. It has the connotation of being unredeemed and solely creaturely, of having fallen out of the divine relationship. Man could not love the world in the Johannine sense (compare 1John 2:15) that 'you must not love this passing world,' since he himself is much too much a part of this world, and participates in its transitory, creaturely nature. First of all he must free himself from it and grasp something within him that 'is not of this world,' that is eternal instead of transitory ('the world with all it craves for, is coming to an end, but anyone who does the will of God, remains forever'). In other words, he must overcome the world, or else the budding power of love within him will turn into love of darkness. Remarkable enough in this same context of the conversation with Nicodemus the passage about God's love for the world is followed by the words, 'and men have shown they prefer darkness to the light' (3:19). Darkness — that is the world seen without its divine foundation, the epitome of the non-eternal, human existence that has been sundered from the divine and become vain and meaningless in this isolation. The love of those men who have not yet become aware of the eternal in them become caught up in this morass. 'The love of the Father cannot be in any man who loves the world' (1John 2:15). In view of the conversation with Nicodemus, one could alter that to say: 'Only if a man had God's love in him could he love the world with true agape.'

Men's 'love of darkness'* is not only insufficient love of the light, but even 'they prefer darkness to the light' (3:19). In the same conversation during the night in which the mystery of divine love is proclaimed, one finds these words about 'hatred.'

Insofar as Christ loved the world redemptively, he did it in terms of John's Gospel, in that the Father and the Father's love were 'in him.' It is never said of him as the Son that he loved the world — that is reserved for the Father. 'The Father is greater than I.' The Son is called redeemer of the world (4:42; compare 3:17; 12:47), who surrenders himself to give it new life (6:33-51). But in order to redeem it, he must 'overcome' it. This is the keystone in the arch of the Farewell Discourses: 'I have conquered the world' (16:33).

This power to overcome must now enter into his disciples. As long as they regard themselves simply as a component part

---

* Out of the five passages in John's Gospel that use agape negatively, there are two that speak of man's natural love as going astray or being diverted. One is here (3:19): 'love of darkness'; the other is (12:43): 'they put honour *[doxa]* from men before the honour *[doxa]* that comes from God.' In the second case man's natural love is not consumed by the darkness but seduced by the glitter of a false light. The love for light is distorted into a love for appearances, which are the nonappearance of the divine. Rudolf Steiner recognized these opposing forces in the polarity of the Luciferic ('false appearance') and the Ahrimanic ('darkness').

of the world, they cannot redeem it. For that reason one may not interpret it as cold indifference to the fate of the world when Christ, in his high priestly prayer, says: 'I pray for them; I am not praying for the world but for those you have given me' (17:9).

In the process of overcoming the world and transforming man, Christ becomes the redeemer of the world. In this simple yet monumental way, it is only about the Father that John says, 'He loved the world.'

The ultimate simplicity of the following proclamation is just as magnificent, 'that he gave his only Son.' The New Testament usually speaks of the Father sending the Son; this is the sole passage in John's Gospel that speaks of the Son being given. The foregoing prophecy of the cross on Golgotha, formulated in the image of the elevated serpent, clearly shows the sacrificial character of this 'giving.'

'Giving' is one of John's basic concepts. Everything which in the further course of the Gospel the Father is said to give is included in this one sentence (3:16) as in its root: he gave his Son. This is a fundamental confrontation between two of the basic concepts of John's Gospel: 'agape' and 'giving.'

The 'night' is the appropriate setting for this revelation. The night of the conversation with Nicodemus is not the night of Judas Iscariot (13:30). Judas' night is darkness, the absence of light. The revelatory conversation penetrates the curtain of darkness to the hidden light that radiates from the sun that 'shines at midnight.'

The only passage about God's love for the world is followed by the only passage in John's Gospel about the 'anger' of God. It is John the Baptist's final word: anyone who refuses to believe in the Son will never see life: the wrath of God stays on him (3:36). This relation of the Father to the world as it is distorted by the Fall is described with the form of wrath which had been preached by the final representatives of the Old Covenant. It strikes one as the outer shell of a deeper mystery that was preached not by the Baptist but by God's only Son:

the mystery of God's love for the world. This mention of anger serves not only as contrast but is like a shell around the words about love; it serves as protection against a cowardly, sentimental understanding of love that lacks austerity and awe in the face of God's holiness.

2. The agape of the Father for the Son

The Father Loves the Son

This consideration of the Baptist's final words leads immediately to the second mention of divine agape (3:35).

The Father loves the Son and has entrusted everything
to him.

The Father 'surrendered' his Son for the salvation of the world because he is interiorly one with him. This giving is a sacrificial act of love because he is not simply giving an external possession, but something intimately bound up with him.

The Synoptic Gospels report the Baptism at the Jordan, when the heavens opened, the dove descended, and a voice was heard from heaven: 'You are my beloved son.' Such a report is missing in John. His account begins at a later point, when the Baptism is already regarded as a past event.

The absence of just such events which one would have thought were particularly close to the heart of the fourth evangelist is altogether surprising. 'Missing' is not only the Baptism but also the Transfiguration, the Last Supper and the Ascension. On closer inspection, however, one may discern that the events missed are still contained in the gospel in some way, albeit in a finer, more 'atmospheric' form, as it were. It seems that the 'corporeality' of a concrete event-related narrative has been sacrificed, liberating in its place something of the inner essence of the event in question, permeating the text like a fragrance.

Thus the first chapter especially gives the impression of

having had something of the *substance of the event at the Jordan* poured into it. This is confirmed by such passages as 'you will see heaven laid open' (1:51) or 'born from above' and 'coming from above' in Chapter 3, not to mention the direct testimony in 1:32-34. Thus the words 'you are my beloved *[agapētos]* Son' have their echo in what the Baptist, who witnesses the baptism at the Jordan, says: 'The Father loves the Son.'

Here again agape is bound up with 'giving.' The sentence quoted is flanked by two others that speak of the Father's giving: 'he whom God has sent speaks God's own words: God gives him the Spirit without reserve.' And he 'entrusted everything to him.'

The divine ground of the universe shows his love for the Son by giving him words of wisdom from the Holy Spirit and power from the Father.

The Father Loves Me

The evangelist has allowed a significant lapse of time before he has Christ himself express his consciousness of being loved by the Father with agape. This gives rise to the impression that it was only gradually that the event at the Jordan developed within Christ's consciousness.

The sentence in 5:20, '... the Father loves the Son and shows him everything he does himself,' serves as a transition from the words of the Baptist, 'the Father loves the Son,' to the passage where Christ says it himself, 'The Father loves me.' But in 5:20 the word used is not *agapa* but *philei*.

Philéein is the other Greek word for 'to love.' To anticipate the result of our subsequent treatment of John 11:5 and 21:15, *philéein* stands underneath *agapē* in the hierarchy of Johannine words. It expresses more personal friendship and affection whereas agape points to a high, majestic form of divine love, which does not exclude this more personal 'liking' but does express something higher. In any case the word *agapē* is not in question in 5:20.

A great deal has yet to happen before Christ's perception of the voice from heaven has sufficiently matured to be expressed in words. Between the Baptism at the Jordan and these words lies nothing less than the greatest portion of Christ's public service, six of the seven miracles that John mentions: the marriage at Cana, the healing of the boy, the healing of the cripple, the feeding of the five thousand, the walking on the lake, and the healing of the man born blind. We are standing between the sixth and seventh miracles, between the healing of the blind man and the raising of Lazarus.

It is the time of the autumn festival (Tabernacles) before the Passover. The words are spoken toward the end of the parable about the good shepherd. The words of Christ spoken in Chapter 10 spread over the autumn (10:1-21) and winter (10:22-39) periods — the Feast of the Dedication of the Temple took place around mid-December — and they receive their peculiar character by standing in this lapse of time, between the sixth and seventh miracles. On the one hand, they refer to the healing of the blind man. As opposed to the loveless treatment shown to the healed man by the priests called to shepherd his people, Christ shows himself to be the Good Shepherd. On the other hand, the approaching raising of Lazarus also casts a special light on these words in Chapter 10. In a very specific sense Christ will show himself as a shepherd to Lazarus. The raising of Lazarus also stands in the closest proximity, chronologically and in its essential meaning, to the death and resurrection of Christ.

Thus the parable about the good shepherd is partly inspired by what is about to come and already contains thoughts about Jesus' free and sovereign sacrificial death. It is in this context that Christ speaks for the first time about the agape of the Father for him: 'The Father loves me because I lay down my life in order to take it up again' (10:17).

He then speaks of the sovereign freedom with which he goes out to meet his death: 'No one takes it from me; I lay it down of my own free will, and as it is in my power to lay it down, so it is in my power to take it up again; and this is the command I have been given by my Father' (10:18). The word 'command' *(entolē)* here must intend something beyond its Old Testament connotations. It must be something like 'a goal to which he has been consecrated' or 'a goal he strives toward spiritually' that the Father has shown him. It is similar to the passage (5:19f), which speaks, in place of charge or commandment, about the Son's looking toward the Father who 'shows' him what he himself is doing. The 'commandment' that the Father gives Christ is such a goal-image that is 'shown' to him.

Dying and rising, self-surrendering and receiving anew, is a law of life grounded in the divine. Through Golgotha and Easter, the Son reveals a mystery within the realm of what man can conceive — a mystery that would otherwise be lost in the depths of the divine brilliance in the night of the blinding light which no one can penetrate.

When Christ speaks of the good shepherd who will give his life for those entrusted to him, he realizes with special clarity that he is the Son of the Father.

The importance of the phrase: 'to commit one s life' is brought out through repetition: 'I am the good shepherd: the good shepherd is one who lays down his life for his sheep' (10:11). '... and I lay down my life for my sheep' (10:15). In 10:17 it is coupled with the reference to the Father's agape: 'The Father loves me because I lay down my life ...'

As is so often the case with John, the order within the Trinity is revealed within the development of the thought: the thought first appears as objective knowledge 'in the third person' (10:11). Then it is expressed personally in the first person (10:15), and finally it is related to the Father (10:17).

Christ is about to fulfill this 'commitment' in an over-whelming intensification now that he approaches the mystery of his death: first, through the raising of Lazarus and, second, through his own resurrection. This drawing closer to death is a progress within John's Gospel and is designated by the reference to the Father's agape for Christ. The Son who is preparing himself 'to go to the Father' grows toward a constantly increasing similarity with the Father. 'I am going to the Father' is not only the most sublime interpretation of the death he is approaching; it also means that in freely taking upon himself this sacrificial death, Christ is drawing decisively closer to the Father. The passage we already mentioned is being fulfilled here: '... the Son can do nothing by himself; he can do what he sees the Father doing: and whatever the Father does, the Son does too. For the Father loves the Son and shows him everything he does himself, and he will show him even greater things than these, works that will astonish you' (5:19f). In carrying out and realizing what has been shown to him, he experiences the Father's love.

This first mention by Christ of the Father's agape for him is the presupposition for the overwhelming revelation that 'The Father and I are one' (10:30).

Undoubtedly a quarter of a year lies between the shepherd parable, which was told at the autumn festival, and these words, which were spoken at the winter feast of the Dedication of the Temple. But that there is a thread uniting the two can be seen in the resumption of the shepherd motif in 10:27. Therefore this statement about 'being one' stands within the radius of the statement about agape; this statement is amazing in that Christ for the first time combines himself with the Father in a 'we' *(esmen,* 'we are,' the first person plural), even though the emphatic 'we' *(hēmeis)* is reserved for the high priestly prayer. His consciousness of the Father's agape being poured out over him enables Christ to say this.

One's attention might be drawn to the appearance of the 'oneness' motif immediately preceding the statement about agape (10:17): 'one flock, and one Shepherd' (10:16). 'Oneness' for John is not merely numerical but connotes a kind of mystical yet personal union. In the immediate vicinity of the agape passage it appears in three different forms: one flock, one shepherd, one *(mia, heis, hen).*

With this consciousness Christ approaches the mystery of his death. The first step is the raising of Lazarus. This sentence, 'The Father loves me,' sets the tone for the whole new portion of the Gospel, which begins with Chapter 11.

The motif is carried on within the Farewell Discourses. In the conclusion to his parable about the vine, Christ says: *'As the Father has loved me, so I have loved you.* Remain in my love' (15:9; since in Greek 'I' and 'my' appear in the emphatic form, we will emphasize them here).

Christ's love for his disciples (which we will discuss in the next chapter) presupposes the Father's love for Christ. Unlike 10:17, the Father's love is not the only thing expressed here. 'The Father loves me' is now woven into a larger context through the Johannine, 'just as.'

It appears within the same context in the following sentence:

> If you keep my commandments you will remain in my
> love, just as I have kept my Father's commandments
> *and remain in his love* (15:10).

Here too, 'just as.' Christ applies to himself the same words as to his disciples: observe the commandments, remain in love. We have already spoken about the word 'commandment' *(entolē).* 'To observe' is more than an external 'keeping.' It is a careful watching and a watchful carefulness; it points to a nurturing of the interior life. It is much more living than a rigid observance of ordinances. Its connotations include faithful 'meditation' and correct action. It designates a reception into the rhythmic course of one's daily life of the divine goal to which one has been consecrated. Inseparable from it is the endurance of pious fidelity and persistence.

In accepting this goal as he does, Christ goes out through his own activity to meet the love being given him. This gives the passage its special character. This time it does not say merely: 'The Father loves me,' but, 'I remain in his love.' It is impossible in a personal relationship for one member to be 'merely an object.' Therefore, Christ relates himself consciously through his activity to the highest gift of grace being given him. In this way it becomes fully his own.

'Remain' belongs among the unfathomable Johannine words. Its meaning stretches from the simplest literal interpretation to the most hidden mystical interpretation. It can mean 'remain, dwell, persist, be eternal.'

Its imperative use, Remain! (15:10), shows that it is bound to an inner activity and, contrary to the first impression, does not refer to something stationary and passive as opposed to the dynamic of movement. Its antonym is not active movement but inactive coming to an end (1John 2:17).

In order to remain in John's sense it requires the expenditure of a powerful interior energy, an interior putting of oneself in motion. It is similar to the word 'observe' *(tērein)* — both words point to a process of life in which one is rhythmically 'breathed through.' One is moved and yet calm within this movement.

In relation to 10:17 and 15:9, this is an important expansion: the Father loves the Son, and the Son makes himself worthy to remain permanently in this state of being loved through constant interior movement and careful observation of the divine goals. In this being loved, he possesses the eternity of his own essence. 'I remain in his love.'

You Loved Me

The high priestly prayer gives a final form to the thought, 'the Father loves the Son.' At the conclusion of this magnificent text the love of the Father for the Son is expressed three times.

I have given them the glory *[doxa]* you gave to me,
that they may be one as we are one. With me in them
and you in me, may they be so completely one that the
world will realize that it was you who sent me and that
I have loved them [the disciples] as much as you loved
me. (17:22f).

The most intimate and personal formulation is reached here. Let us look back at the previous passages: 'The Father loves the Son'; 'the Father loves me'; 'I remain in his love'; 'you love me.'

Thus at the conclusion of Christ's earthly life the perfect reflection is attained of the words spoken at the Baptism in the Jordan: 'You are my beloved Son.' This occurs in the third part of the high priestly prayer. After Christ first prays for his own glorification and for that of the apostles, he broadens his scope and prophetically includes the growing Church, the future Christian humanity.

As in the tenth chapter, the chapter about the good shepherd, the notion of 'one' (a neuter in Greek, *hen; unum* in Latin) reappears here and is once again placed in relation to the divine plural 'we'; here, however, it stands as a climax.

This 'one' has a special intonation in John's Gospel. The word is a neuter, an 'it.' Through a transition from the personal, which corresponds to the dignity of man, to the nonpersonal 'it,' language can express descent in the hierarchy. For example, one might point with scorn to a man, by using the words, 'that thing.' There is, however, the reverse possibility. One can also say of a man that he is 'something very great.' Then the neuter expression intends something very high that is not beneath but above that which we usually refer to as the personal language. This is the case in the Annunciation to Mary in Luke's Gospel: 'The holy that you will bear shall be called Son of God.'* This 'the holy' (neuter in Greek) pushes language to its limit and tries through this neuter to intimate something unspeakably high. Thus the Johannine 'one' is also to be placed beyond the everyday personal.

The 'one' motif appears for the first time in John's Gospel during the Feast of Tabernacles. Christ has given light to the man born blind. The repeated appearance of the words 'see,' 'know,' and 'recognize' within this chapter that encompasses the Feast of Tabernacles indicates that something more is being spoken of than eyesight (7:1-10:21). Gradually the eyes of the

---

* The Jerusalem Bible has: 'And so the child will be holy.'

healed man are opened so that he can see his healer. He who has learned to see must hold fast to his understanding in the face of his fellow man's doubts and resistance and even in the face of the enmity of the Pharisees who are supposed to be his shepherd. This insistence on his personal experience can be maintained only at the cost of total isolation. He is turned out of the synagogue. In view of this isolation Christ begins to speak of the new personal community of those who have become free through knowledge and over which he will be the 'Good Shepherd.' His relation to those who follow him, he expresses as follows: 'I am the good shepherd; I know my own and my own know me, just as the Father knows me and I know the Father' (10:14f). The presupposition for the new community Christ is founding is the opening of eyes, knowledge, and the freeing of the individual. It is not until then that the words *'one* flock, and *one* shepherd' are spoken. The first 'one' in 10:30 refers to the relationship between God the Father and God the Son. In 11:52, the evangelist allows this 'one' to fall from above to our level and to be applied to man. After that it appears in the sacred context of the high priestly prayer. If we follow the apparently more reliable reading, according to which it appears only once in 17:21, it is used five times in the prayer: (17:11, 12, 21, 22, 23). Therefore, together with 10:30 and 11:52, it becomes one of those phrases that John uses seven times.

The words in 17:21, 'May they all be one' *(Ut omnes unum sint* in Latin), do not intend the 'one' to apply to an external organization and have nothing to do with what would be called in the language of power politics a 'monolithic block.' Because of its connection to the relation between God the Father and God the Son ('just as'), the 'being one' becomes something infinitely sublime and of a divine character; man will not achieve it before his future 'perfection' (17:23).

In the high priestly prayer, the two series of passages about 'oneness' and 'love' are definitely fused.

'That they may be one like us' (17:11) appears in the first

part of the prayer. The main passage, however, is in the second part: 'May they all be one ... may they be one in us ... that they may be one as we are one' (17:22), 'may they be completely one' (17:23).

In relation to 10:30, the divine plurality is expressed with unusual force in that the emphatic form of 'we' *(hērmeis)* is used. It appears three times with reference to God in Chapter 17 (17:11,21,22). This is without parallel in the rest of the Gospel. The 'I' is surpassed here by the 'we.' Once again the key to the 'one' and to the 'we' is agape. Seeing the Trinitarian love between the Father, Christ, and the Church, the world is to be brought not only to faith in the mission of Christ (17:21) but to a knowledge as well: 'so ... that the world will realize.' The world will know not only that Christ has been sent by the Father but also that 'you have loved the world just as you have loved me.'

The veil that has hidden the divine from the world until now will be removed in the future. The appearance of the Trinity, which breaks into the human realm in the Church, causes the presence of the divine on earth to become so obvious that it can be known — even by 'the world.' This must, however, be preceded by a powerful realization of the divine in man. By the way in which Christians manifest their 'being loved by God' a window is opened for the world so that it can actually know something of that transcendent mystery within God 'as much as you loved me.'

The next sentence shows this love to have existed before creation: '... so that they may always see the glory you have given me *because you loved me before the foundation of the world'* (17:24, emphasis added).

John causes us to look through the words spoken at the Baptism in the Jordan and see an eternal mystery. Christ had already spoken (17:5) of his glory *(doxa)*, a revealing, radiating brightness which he had before the world was with God. When *doxa* is spoken of again in 17:22 and 17:24 the phrase, 'which I had' is replaced by 'you gave to me.' Friedrich Rittelmeyer often pointed out (compare his writing on John's Gospel) how, in the high priestly prayer, 'my own' is for the most part replaced by *'which you gave me.'* He drew attention to the way in which this transfigured the 'my own.' 'The work, that you gave me' (17:4); 'the men ... you gave ... to me' (17:6); 'the teaching you gave to me' (17:8); 'the glory you gave to me' (17:22). It is significant that in this final reference to the *doxa* of Christ (it is the last within John's Gospel), the words 'my own' should nevertheless reappear. The way in which 'my own' and 'which you gave to me' are combined with one another in this passage is unique. The key to this is agape: '... so that they may always see [emphatic form in Greek] the glory you have given me because you loved me before the foundation of the world.'

'My own' is purged of all egotism and made selfless and transparent by means of this reference to its original 'givenness' by God. On the other hand, 'you gave to me' becomes clear in all its seriousness in this 'my own': it is a thoroughly real giving in which the giver divorces himself totally from his gift in order that it may fully belong to the receiver.

This is the ultimate conquest over Lucifer: radiant glory combining the two qualifiers 'my own' and 'you have given me.' As in 3:16, the agape motif is here again joined with that of 'giving' in a fundamental relationship.

Just as the Johannine agape-context in the high priestly prayer is brought into contact with the other contexts of 'one,' 'we,' and 'giving,' so too, as we have seen, with the *doxa* context. *Doxa* is one of the most important Johannine words. The history of this concept of the *doxa* of Christ in the Fourth Gospel stretches all the way from the Prologue ('we saw his glory,' 1:14) to this passage ('so that they may always see the glory you have given me,' 17:24). This final passage resounds together with the first.

The final passage in this series is the concluding sentence of the high priestly prayer. 'I have made your name known to them and will continue to make it known, so that the love with which you loved me may be in them and so that I may be in them' (17:26).

Even here at the conclusion of the prayer, the truth of the Father's agape for the Son does not stand in isolation. The way it was woven in to the 'just-as' sentences (15:9f; 17:23) has already shown that it does not want to stand alone. This not-standing-alone is intensified in this final passage (17:26), even though the thought 'you have loved me' is placed in a modest relative clause. This construction is by no means intended to relativize the reality. It shows that this agape is in the fullest sense not to remain 'exclusive,' but rather, in the receiver's opinion, ought to be mediated. This again reveals the opposition between Christ's essence and Lucifer's. He regards this highest gift as something he cannot keep to himself. The emphasis in this sentence is on the desire of the Father's love to be in the disciples. His own reception of this love serves only as a background. For that very reason, this passage is the apogee of the series of passages we are now able to survey. It is precisely in its stepping back, in its unwillingness to be a final goal sought for its own sake, that this agape reveals its dignity.

3. The agape of the Father for the disciples

The Father's agape is directed toward the world, the Son, and the disciples. In the order in which they are mentioned the disciples are the third object of the Father's love.

The entire first part of the Gospel does not give them this honour; the first reference is in the Farewell Discourses. It is also significant that in all these passages about the Father's love for the disciples, it is always spoken of as something future, as something that has yet to be brought to them. Obviously the reference here must be to a special meaning of agape. The Father's general love for the disciples does not need to be

realized in the future. We are here concerned with a special
kind of agape. If the disciples have not yet received it, it can
only be because they have not yet developed sufficiently to
participate in it. The love given them up until now is the one
mentioned in 3:16 ('loved the world'). Not until they have
been awakened can they raise themselves above this world.

Chapter 14

The first passage is in the fourteenth chapter. In 14:16 Christ
has promised, for the first time, the coming of the Holy Spirit
as a consoler. He then (14:18) spoke of his own return, and of
the higher life to which the disciples are called, but which they
have not yet begun: 'you will live' (14:19).

> Anybody who receives my commandments and keeps
> them will be one who loves me; and anybody who
> loves me *will be loved by my Father* ... (14:21, empha-
> sis added).

One is struck by the passive form, 'will be loved'; it is the
only one in John's Gospel. This unusual mode of expression,
occurring precisely at the point where a new thought is introduced, is bound to have a special significance. It could mean
'will be able' (in this higher, special sense) to be loved by the
Father. Through their disposition they are enabled to absorb the
rays that up until now more or less passed over them. Because
their love for Christ has proved itself in action, they have made
themselves worthy objects of this highest agape.

Immediately after this passage the thought reappears but in
a different formulation:

> If anyone loves me he will keep my word, and *my
> Father will love him* ... (14:23, emphasis added).

Once again an active love for Christ is presupposed. This
time the active form is used, 'my Father will love him.' Here
the future experience, also mentioned in 14:21, is more God's.
It expresses something unusual. God the Father, who is the
first beginning from eternity, will make a new beginning. His
eternity is not stagnant. It does not exclude but specifically

includes the possibility that God will move on to new possibilities — because of the Christian's maturing. This could be somewhat clarified by an example: one shows a different love toward a child from what one does toward an adult. In order to receive the love that an adult is capable of receiving a man must first have matured to adulthood. Likewise there is a special kind of divine love for the mature man, but God must retain it until a man is ready for it. This is a human comparison, but anthropomorphisms are not false in principle; after all, man's fundamental direction is 'theomorphic.'

The passive form in 14:21 had more the meaning: when he becomes aware of it, man will open himself to something that is already present (until now it had not been brought to his attention). The active form in 14:23 brings a new nuance: God's will to do something new, something that was previously nonexistent. The present-tense verb in 16:27, 'for the Father himself loves you,' is not a contradiction because it is *philei* (not *agapei*). Perhaps, however, we are being too rigid to talk of such a delicate matter in this way; perhaps the sensitivity needed to perceive this love cannot be expressed in words.

These passages (14:21-23) end as they began: with a promise of the Holy Spirit: 'the Advocate, the Holy Spirit, whom the Father will send in my name' (14:26). Thus this promise that the Father will show man a special love that he could not show previously is enclosed by two promises to send the Holy Spirit, who will be active among Christians. Within the Godhead the Holy Spirit represents the future aspect.

The high priestly prayer

Turning from Chapter 14 to the high priestly prayer, we find that the concluding sentences of the prayer also lead into the sphere of the Holy Spirit, the future 'Church':

... that the world will realize that it was you who sent me and that I have loved them as much as you loved me (17:23).

Looking out beyond the present apostles, Christ prays for those who will come to believe in him through the preaching of the apostles. The glory *(doxa)* of Christ should radiate from them in such a way that the world can perceive that the Father's agape is being poured out upon them. The concluding 'as' places the future Christians alongside the Son. The words spoken at the Baptism in the Jordan apply to them as well. What John intimated in his First Letter will be fulfilled: '... what we are to be in the future has not been revealed; all we know is, that when it is revealed we shall be like him ...' (1John 3:2).

As unbelievably bold as the prophecy in 17:23 is, it is surpassed in the concluding sentence of the high priestly prayer:

So that the love with which you have loved me may be in them and so that I *may be in them'* (17:26).

This surpasses the 'as' insofar as it expresses a total identity of agape. The very same love with which the Father loved Christ should be 'in them.' This is an absolute climax. 'In them' means that the Father's agape is no longer something that comes from without and merely externally touches man's essence; it is fully received and made a part of man;* it will

---

* The passage 5:42 is the 'negative side' of this crowning conclusion of the high priestly prayer: 'I know you too well: you have no love of God in you *[en heautois].'* The two passages are related as *emptiness* and *fulfilment.* Without the in-pouring of divine agape, the human personality remains an empty cup. It is not only in their contents that 5:42 and 17:26 stand in a polar relation to one another. The noun 'agape' appears seven times in John's Gospel and it appears that these passages, aside from being in the larger contexts that we have already pointed out, also combine with one another to form a sevenfold organism, listed here:

1. '... you have no love of God in you' (5:42).
   2. '... this you have love for one another' (13:35).
      3. 'Remain in my love, ...' (15:9).
         4. '... you will remain in my love' (15:10).
      5. '... and remain in his love' (15:10).
   6. 'A man can have no greater love ...' (15:13).
7. '... that the love with which you have loved me may be in them' (17:26).

The words about emptiness and fullness stand in the first and last of these seven passages. In this sevenfold series is also a crowning conclusion (17:26).

become one in a final communion with man's self *(en autois,* 'in their very selves'). This is the mystical, Johannine 'in' that appears for the last time in John's Gospel at the end of the high priestly prayer. The series of agape passages converges at this point with the high point of another Johannine series, which is characterized by the mystical 'in.'

It is certainly no accident that John, on the one hand, is the evangelist of the 'I am' statements and, on the other hand, so frequently uses the word 'in.' The self-contained character of the personality is inseparably bound up with the 'I am.' The personality powerfully comprises itself within itself and is distinguished from all other beings. If the personality succumbs to egotism, the character of self-containedness becomes one of isolation, of being caught and imprisoned in oneself. If the ego makes itself into a bearer of love, it is capable of selflessly and yet personally moving over into another's being with full consciousness. Likewise it can invite foreign being into its interior and, as Novalis phrased it, 'receive it within.' The self-contained character of the person is not a goal in itself, but the presupposition for free disposition over oneself; only he who fully possesses himself can fully give himself. The ego that is capable of living in the other and of taking the other into itself is capable of interiority.

It is important to notice how 'knowledge' and 'love' are united with one another at the conclusion of Chapter 17. The Father's agape will be able to be in the disciples because Christ reveals the Father's name to them more and more clearly. This emphasis on knowledge also leads into the realm of the Holy Spirit. In comparing passages 17:23-26 and 14:21-23, one notices among other things that Chapter 14 speaks of the individual man who opens himself to the Father's agape through active love for Christ. 'Anybody who receives my commandments and keeps them' — '... anybody who loves me.' The transformation begins in the individual. The individual Christianized ego is then allowed to recognize itself more and more in the great 'we.' The high priestly prayer, as

distinct from the fourteenth chapter, speaks of the many who
will become one community ('one'): 'that you have loved
them ...,' 'that love is ... in them.' In the person of the
individuals who have been interiorly awakened, this community is also ruled over by the Holy Spirit.

24. The agape of the Son

1. The agape of the Son for his own

In the survey at the beginning we saw that in the first ten chapters only the Father is said to practice true agape. To declare the Son a bearer of agape as well shows his increasing transfiguration. This is done for the first time in the story about Lazarus.

Lazarus

It is to some extent prepared for in the previous chapter, where Christ says for the first time that he knows he is loved by the Father with agape (10:17). These words at the end of the first half of the Gospel serve as a transition to the word at the beginning of the second half:

Jesus loved Martha and her sister and Lazarus (11:5).

The beginning of the new division at Chapter 11 is indicated by the concluding verses of Chapter 10 (40-42), which recall the activity of the Baptist near the Jordan. On the other hand, one could also rightfully claim that the major division, which divides the Gospel into clearly distinct parts if not into two 'halves,' lies between chapters 12 and 13. The conclusion to Chapter 12 resembles an epilogue, and the beginning of Chapter 13 a prologue, which introduces the washing of the feet and the sacred realm of the Farewell Discourses. That in turn puts us in immediate proximity to the mystery of Golgotha.

Nevertheless, it is still not false to place the major division before the Lazarus chapter. The difficulties one has in trying to assign the raising of Lazarus to either the first or second part of the Gospel indicate the twofold role of the chapter.

It belongs to the first half insofar as the raising of Lazarus concludes and crowns the series of the seven miracles reported in John's Gospel. It is the conclusion of Christ's externally directed activity.

It belongs to the second half insofar as the raising of Lazarus stands in the narrower realm of the mystery of Golgotha. Just looking at the external chronological aspect, it is necessary to see this event as quite close to Easter. It is also closely related to the death of Christ in that the High Council was moved by reports of the event at Bethany to make the final decision to kill Jesus (11:50). In John's Gospel the exaltation of the people during Christ's entrance into Jerusalem is motivated by their knowledge of his raising of Lazarus (12:17).

But the relation is even more intimate. Through the raising of Lazarus, Christ becomes aware of his own power to rise from the dead — a power hidden in the depths of his being. He experiences the power of Easter at the grave of Lazarus. 'I am the resurrection and the life.' Thus the awakening of Lazarus belongs intimately to the events of Golgotha and Easter. Friedrich Rittelmeyer once expressed it this way, that Christ needed to raise someone from the dead in order to be able to rise up himself, in order to approach his own death with a consciousness of having overcome death. In this respect the story of Lazarus belongs more to the second than to the first half of the Gospel. This is true also from the point of view of John's statements about agape.

The sisters have sent their message, 'Lord, the man you love [*phileis*] is ill' (11:3). Christ answers with the overwhelming interpretation: 'This sickness will end, not in death ...' This is followed immediately by the evangelist's comment: 'Jesus loved [*agape*] ...' The two words for love, *philein* and *agapein,* are placed right next to each other. The order of precedence cannot be overlooked. The sisters speak of 'having affection' just as the Jews do at the grave: 'See how much he loved him' (11:36).

It is as if the evangelist wanted gently to correct what the sisters said. He knows that Christ loves Lazarus in an even deeper and more divine way than the sisters can intimate. They appeal to his *philein* but in reality he was already showing *agapē* 'above and beyond their desire and understanding.'

The key to the transition from *philia* to *agapē* lies in the words of Christ that unite the two passages: 'This sickness will end, not in death, but in God's glory [glorification, revelation — *doxa* in the Greek], through which the Son of God will be glorified' (11:4). This may not be interpreted in the superficial sense to mean that Lazarus has to die in order for Christ to have the opportunity to show his miraculous power. To put it bluntly, there were plenty of other dead people for Christ to awaken. It was not a question of just anyone but specifically of Lazarus, for whom he 'had affection,' whom he called 'Our friend, Lazarus' (11:11). Lazarus had to be someone for whom this dying and being raised would have a very special meaning. There were other dead for whom relatives and friends mourned, but Christ did not raise anyone else after four days. This is one consideration that could help us to appreciate Rudolf Steiner's interpretation of this as a 'death of initiation.' The words spoken at the grave side, 'I am the resurrection. If anyone believes in me, even though he die, he will live ...' show that he is speaking not of an external revivification but of a rebirth from the dead.

This would remove our indignation at Christ's strange, seemingly callous delay after receiving the message. (When he heard that Lazarus was ill, he stayed where he was for two more days, before saying to his disciples, 'Let us go to Judea'; 11:6f.) He did not delay in order that his miracle might appear all the more wonderful because he raised up someone dead for several days, but in order for the three and a half days of the death of initiation to pass. The attempt has been made to see in this delay a psychological proof for the falsity of the

Johannine Christ: How could that be the merciful Saviour if he ignores the pain of the sisters and is concerned only with proving his divinity through the most spectacular miracle possible? All of these accusations would be justified if we were concerned here only with the revivification of a dead man; they are refuted, however, if we look at the event as an initiation. This could happen not to just any dead man but only to someone who was close to Christ.

If Christ had only *philia* for Lazarus and his sisters, he would have spared them the death and the sorrow — but in so doing, he would have withheld the mystery of the resurrection from them. He allowed Lazarus to die and raised him because he loved him with *agapē,* with a love that was concerned with Lazarus' eternal life and its development. *Agapē* reveals here its magnificent austerity and majesty.

This clarifies the short sentence (11:5) inserted by the evangelist. It makes Christ's seemingly callous behaviour understandable and places the right sign before the entire event.

The agape sequence merges here with the other Johannine sequence of *doxa.* The sickness was not intended to end in death but to provide the occasion for a greater revelation of the divine; it was 'for the *doxa* of God.' It is put even more explicitly, '... through it the Son of God will be glorified' *(doxasthē).*

The raising from the dead brought greater glory to the Son of God not only in the person of Jesus of Nazareth but likewise in Lazarus. Shortly afterwards John writes that he sat at the same table with the Lord (12:2), which is to be interpreted in the sense of 'and in them I am glorified' (17:10).

We have already referred to the Transfiguration as an account that is 'lacking' in John's Gospel — yet constitutes the delicate atmosphere of the entire Gospel. What in the Synoptics is a single isolated event on Mount Tabor has been developed in John to the grand sequence of *doxa* passages, which begins even in the Prologue ('we saw his glory'). In

John's view Christ had his divine glory from the very beginning of his activity. After the first miracle at Cana, John writes: 'He let his glory be seen' (2:11), but this glory is more hidden in the beginning. Its full majesty appears more and more fully as Golgotha and Easter approach. Thus, in spite of the statement about Cana (2:11), the evangelist can write in the seventh chapter, 'because Jesus had not yet been glorified' (7:39), and likewise in 12:16.

The statement in 11:4 'that through it [the sickness] the Son of God will be glorified' introduces something new into John's Gospel. The transfiguration and glorification that will occur at Golgotha and Easter begin here with the raising of Lazarus.

It should be noticed that in 11:4 John speaks of the glorification of the Son of *God,* and in 12:23 and 13:31 of the glorification of the Son of *Man.* The glorification comes from above and penetrates into the earthly more and more deeply. First the form of the Son of God begins to radiate more brightly and later Christ's human nature becomes more luminous.

The mystery of Bethany glorifies the Son of God and the mystery of Golgotha the Son of Man.

John's first reference to Christ's agape (in 11:5) is made more meaningful by this context. It follows immediately the words about glorification: '... but in God's glory, and through it the Son of God will be glorified.'

The sequence 'Jesus loved Martha and her sister and Lazarus' contains an intensification. Martha has the most distant relation to the event, Mary is more sensitive to his agape, and Lazarus experiences it most decisively of all. This likewise interprets the sequence of scenes at Bethany: the first meeting is with Martha (11:20). the second with Mary (11:32). and the third with Lazarus.

Perhaps it is also worth noticing that the Father's love is first referred to by the Son (3:16) and the Son's love by the evangelist (11:5).

The motif of Christ's love for the men who belong to him

and whom he wants to lead to a higher life develops in the second part of the Gospel.

At the beginning of the washing of the feet

At the beginning of the thirteenth chapter, which introduces the reader to the inner sanctuary of the Farewell Discourses by means of the account of the washing of the feet, the evangelist speaks of the agape of Christ with great solemnity:

It was before the festival of the Passover, and Jesus knew that the hour had come for him to pass from this world to the Father. He had always loved those who were his in the world, but now he showed how perfect his love was. (13:1)

Looking back, the author places all that Christ had done under the radiance of the word 'agape.' 'He had always loved those who were his in the world, ...' This is a continuation of the sequence begun in 11:5. But the following is immediately presented as an intensification, in that the word 'love' is united with the expression *telos* (in the Mysteries, *telos* meant the final stage of initiation): 'he loved them till the end,' till the end of the initiation. *Telos* is also contained in the word spoken from the Cross: *'telestai'* (19:30), 'It is accomplished.'

This 'love till the end' is related to his 'leaving this world and going to the Father,' to his being fully consecrated by his free surrender of himself into the bosom of the Father.

The sentence in 13:1 is not only a solemn introduction to the washing of the feet, but also a significant prologue to the mystery of Golgotha. It is the heading for the most important part of John's Gospel, which begins here.

From the thirteenth chapter on, it is possible to distinguish two different continuations of the newly begun sequence, 'Christ's agape for his own.' On the one hand, we find this agape spoken of as before by the evangelist 'in the third person.' These four passages about the beloved disciple added to the three references already mentioned in 11:5 and 13:1 add up to a sevenfold sequence.

On the other hand, a second sevenfold sequence begins after the washing of the feet, and in it Christ expresses his love for his own 'in the first person.' We will begin with the words about the beloved disciple.

The beloved disciple

The first mention of the 'apostle, whom the Lord loved' appears at a very dramatic moment.

The washing of the feet has been completed. In deep agitation, 'He was troubled in spirit' (13:21); this is the third and last time that John uses *tarassō* in reference to Christ. Previously it appeared in 12:27 'now my soul is troubled' *(tetaraktai),* which is much stronger than 'depressed.' Its first use was in 11:33, at Lazarus' grave, 'in great distress.'

The earthquake on Good Friday and Easter Sunday mentioned in Matthew's Gospel is anticipated interiorly by Jesus and he is shaken in body, soul, and spirit. Christ has said, 'One of you will betray me.' This dreary background gives special relief to the first reference to the beloved disciple (13:23).

The disciple Jesus loved was reclining next to Jesus*

The word for bosom, *kolpos,* is also used in the Prologue (1:18): God's only Son, who is nearest to the Father's heart. *Kolpos* is the sphere of the heart's inspiration. Just as God's only Son came from his Father's heart as one consecrated to reveal the Father's most intimate love, so the beloved disciple was allowed to receive the inspiration of Christ's heart and become his most prominent herald.

The communion of the beloved disciple with Christ contrasts glaringly with Judas' communion with Satan. Like a stroke of lightning this scene reveals the two ultimate possibilities for a human being: either union with Christ or possession by Satan. Into Judas 'Satan had entered' (13:27).

* Some translations use 'bosom.'

At the beginning of the thirteenth chapter is written: Christ loved his own with agape. And suddenly a specific one of the Twelve is to be specially characterized as 'the one whom Jesus loved.' If the verb 'philein' had been used here, the statement would not be so unusual. In that case it would simply refer to a special personal friendship for one person in addition to his general agape for all. In 20:2 we are told that such a special friendship did also exist, for the reference is to the disciple for whom he had affection *(ephilei)*. But how can it be that precisely Christ's agape should explicitly single out the disciple from the others? Once again the word must have a special meaning here, too. It is similar to 14:23, 'my Father will love him,' which apparently refers to a special love that man generally is not yet capable of receiving. We have already seen that the more a recipient ceases to be a mere 'object' of agape, and the more he becomes an active subject, the more intensely divine agape can encounter him. For example, a man has an endlessly deeper appreciation for God's agape for him than a stone does, which is also an object of God's agape. Likewise, there are various degrees of openness among men. John was the most *awakened* among the apostles; Christ's agape had to be a different experience for him than for the others who in comparison were 'sleeping' disciples.

The fact that the expression 'the beloved disciple' does not appear until after the raising of Lazarus is, among others, an intimate confirmation of Rudolf Steiner's explanation. He claims that John, the author of the Fourth Gospel, hides himself behind the figure of Lazarus who has undergone the mystery of death and resurrection. This would enable John to become a specially initiated herald of Christ.

The Master's agape was given to everyone (13:1), but John alone received it as one who had been awakened. For that reason it meant so much to him that he could justifiably be distinguished from the others as the disciple whom Jesus loved. Christ could reveal to him the depths of his person. John alone would record the Farewell Discourses.

John was the only disciple to stand under the cross on Golgotha (19:26):

Seeing his mother and the disciple he loved standing near her, Jesus said ...

The awakened disciple beholds the mystery of death for the sake of love. He recognizes the sacrifice of the cross as a deed of agape. It produces the agape of the Father who surrenders his only Son (3:16); it produces the agape of the Son who loves both his Father (14:31) and his own till the end (13:1).

Just as he recognized the crucified Christ before the other disciples, so too does he recognize the risen Christ. After the miraculous catch of fish, he sees the risen Christ standing on the shore of Lake of Genesareth. He speaks the first words of recognition.

The disciple Jesus loved said to Peter, 'It is the Lord' *[ho kyrios estin].* (21:7)

This story of the catch of fish and the meeting in the morning on the shore strikes one very much like a dream, and that is what constitutes its unique fascination. If one removed John's words of recognition, the scene would pass before us like a marvellous morning dream which definitely moves the soul in an unusual way yet leaves behind an uncertainty as to whether it is a fabric woven of remembered images or a factual, real meeting with a being out of the supersensible world. When John speaks his words of recognition, a flash of intuition breaks through the obscurity. The fabrication of dreams reveals itself as a true image. In the glimmer of this obscure, early morning experience an absolutely certain truth is grasped.

It is the Lord. Friedrich Rittelmeyer pointed out that this sentence, which in the original has the connotation of 'the Lord is,' occurs three times in the story of the catch of fish. (Rittelmeyer also pointed out that these words in the concluding chapter of the Gospel, 'the Lord is' have the effect of a sealing and confirmation of all the previous 'I am' statements.) The second time is 'At these words, ... Simon Peter ...' (21:7).

The third time: '... None of the disciples was bold enough to ask, "Who are you?" They knew it was the Lord' (21:12). This knowledge originated in John. Peter heard it first and in the end all the disciples realized it. This is followed by the eating of bread and fish, the account of which is stylized like the Feeding of the Five Thousand and thus like the words of the Last Supper (21:13).

As we see the beloved disciple in a special relation to the crucified Christ (19:26) and to the risen Christ (21:7) so the last of these passages (20:2) uses *ephilei,* as we have said, relating to the return of Christ. After the meal on the shore of the lake,

> Peter turned and saw the disciple Jesus loved following
> them — the one who had leaned on his breast at the
> supper and had said to him, 'Lord, who is it that will
> betray you?' Seeing him, Peter said to Jesus, 'What
> about him, Lord?' Jesus answered, 'I want him to stay
> behind till I come, what does it matter to you? You are
> to follow me.' (21:20-22).

The last mention of the beloved disciple refers to the first one. It recalls again the scene at the Last Supper, his reclining close to Jesus and his question about the traitor. The Gospel text does not mention the scene a second time simply to refresh the memory of the forgetful reader. By means of the repetition it illuminates the great mission that has been assigned to John. 'I want him to stay behind till I come' (21:22).

This already refers to the Apocalypse. The remaining (a superficial misunderstanding is explicitly corrected, 21:23) refers to a level of interior life that John has now reached, to a light that has been enkindled in him, that has not been obscured by denial (Peter), nor extinguished by treason (Judas). John's task is to carry this light through a darkened world until the sunrise of Christ's return. In a way he has anticipated its light and represents the future form of Christianity.

The words spoken in the 'first person'

After the washing of the feet, during the course of the Farewell Discourses, Christ expresses his agape for his disciples in direct address. This occurs seven times between chapters 13 and 15.

The washing of the feet has been completed. The night has taken the traitor to herself. Jesus devotes himself now to his disciples with a special intimacy. Indicative of this devotion is the unique use in John's Gospel of the words 'little children' *(teknia;* 21:5 uses the word *paidia).* He uses this word to express to his disciples something germinal, something underway, something to be fulfilled in the future; in spite of all their imperfection he sees in them a beginning of their new birth out of God, by which they will become, as the Prologue says, children of God (1:12). The use of the dimunitive 'little child' expresses how tender and in need of care this seed in them still is. A little child needs warming love without which it cannot grow.

Immediately after Judas' exit, Christ's glory shines forth majestically. 'Now has the Son of Man been glorified ...' (13:31). Clothed with the radiant cloak of his glory, Jesus gives his 'commandment of love' and confirms it with a reference to his own agape for the disciples:

... just as I have loved you (13:34).

He also refers to the other form of agape which is given not to the little child but to the mature. We spoke of this passage in another context.

Anybody who receives my commandments and keeps
them will be one who loves me; and anybody who
loves me will be loved by my Father, and *I shall love
him* and show myself to him (14:21, emphasis added).

This is not said about the agape he has already given; it is prophecy, apocalyptic. The appearance of a new Christian humanity will give both the Father and the Son a new possibility — a future experience for God! He will be able to communicate himself to those who have sufficiently matured by means of an agape that has not yet been manifested in the course of the world's development. In regard to this passage, we have already said that it is given added significance by being placed between two promises of the Holy Spirit (14:16,26).

Corresponding to this future epoch of the Holy Spirit, the prophesied revelation of love is something bright and visible, enlightening and revelatory. 'I shall love him and show myself [emphatic in the original, *emauton*] to him.' This prophecy has already begun to fulfil itself in regard to John.

The other five passages are in Chapter 15. They are all closely grouped together in reference to the metaphor of the vine and the branches. The mood of the fifteenth chapter is that of the Last Supper; it is filled with the mystery of the Eucharist. The following words are condensed out of this atmosphere of communion:

As the Father has loved me, *so I have loved you. Remain in my love.'* (15:9).

If you keep my commandments *you will remain in my love,* just as I have kept my Father's commandments and remain in his love ... (15:10).

This is my commandment: love one another, as I have *loved you* (15:12).

A man can have *no greater love* than to lay down his life for his friends' (15:13, emphasis added).

One should recall that in the entire first half of the Gospel there are not more than three references to true agape and then only to the Father's love. Keeping that in mind, one can better appreciate the uniqueness of this context where the agape of Christ is spoken of again and again and placed in relation to the agape of the Father and the disciples.

This love for his own is like the 'interior' of what the other evangelists describe as the institution of the Eucharist.

Christ's love for his own was presented as the standard for the disciples' love for one another (13:34), and here it is itself measured by the standard of a 'just as': 'just as the Father loved me.' This 'just as' applies also to the 'remaining in love.' The 'remaining in me'* spoken in the parable of the vine (15:3-7) is transformed into a 'remain in my love.' As we have already seen, this is a formulation that grants to the 'object' of agape an activity of its own and thereby elevates it above being a mere object.

Christ speaks here twice of 'remaining in his love.' That occurs in 15:9 in the form of the imperative, 'Remain!' which expresses the active work aspect of this remaining. In 15:10 this activity is then further defined as 'keeping the commandments' and assuming the sacred goals of Christ with great perseverance. It is only through this activity that the disciples can hope to maintain themselves in the reception of his love.

A further difference between 15:9 and 15:10 is the emphatic 'my love' *(eme)* in 15:9. This emphatic 'my' is difficult to translate into English. It appears frequently in John's writings, for instance, 'my peace' and 'my joy.' He expresses the thorough relation of something to Christ's 'ego.' The emphatic 'my' corresponds to the 'I am.' Thus 'my peace' is the peace that is not to be expected from without, from the world, but gives itself from within, from the ego of Christ. Thus the personal character of Christ's agape is especially emphasized in 15:9. This has nothing to do with any kind of egotism; rather, in the way in which Christ's ego presents itself lies the complete victory over egotism. The ego does not withdraw selfishly into itself, but in full, sovereign freedom makes out of itself a grail of divine love.

Precisely because this agape emerges out of the 'I am,' it

---

* This 'remaining in Christ' is spoken of for the first time in the chapter about the feeding with bread in addition to the chapter about the vine from which wine is produced: 'lives in me and I live in him' (6:56). Bread and wine! The evangelist uses the formulation 'remain in Christ' specifically in the 'Eucharistic' contexts of Chapters 6 and 15. In addition one might mention that this motif which occurs first in 6:56, develops into a sevenfold sequence in Chapter 15 (15:3-10)

desires to be received by the disciples in the sphere of the conscious, active, 'lasting' ego.

In 15:12 the phrase from the account of the washing of the feet reappears. This is not a merely external repetition ('monotonous'), but has a specific turn to it after the preceding (15:9): 'as the Father has loved me.' Thus the links of the chain mesh together in the chapter with the vine metaphor: 'just as the Father loved ... so I you. Just as I you ... so you one another.' The series of passages about Christ's agape for his disciples reaches its climax in the thirteenth verse, 'a man can have no greater love ...'

In the ancient sacred texts the word 'great' usually has more or less 'magical' connotation (in the sense of a force that comes from the spiritual and 'moves the world'). The greatest love is simultaneously that which is most effective, which has the highest potency of 'white magic.' 'Black magic' acquires its potency through the sacrifice of another's life. 'White' gives its own life.

'To surrender one's soul [psychē]' — this formulation is familiar to us from the chapter about the good shepherd where it is, in significant repetition, applied to Christ. Its third appearance is in relation to the Father's agape (10:17). Here, in 15:13, it is related to agape in an ultimate, classical way. Christ interprets his death as a deed of the 'greatest love.'

It is unjustifiable to compare this sentence with the exhortation to love one's enemies, in the Sermon on the Mount, and to declare that love 'even greater.' The attempt has been made to prove in this way that the 'Johannine Christ' is a constructed form and does not attain the stature of the true 'Synoptic Christ.' The 'greater' in 15:13 does not refer to the object of the love, to the friends. That definitely could be surpassed. It refers to the way in which the love is shown: through the sacrifice of one's own life. No form of love can surpass that which reveals itself through self-sacrifice.

2. The agape of the Son for the Father

We see repeatedly that John does not place the divine persons in an 'equality' as abstract dogma does. As unequivocally as the divinity of Jesus is proclaimed, just as clearly is the Father said to be greater.

To bring out the incomparable character of the Father's majesty, the reader should realize that in no place — to anticipate for a moment — does John speak of the disciples' love for the Father, not even as a possibility or as a command, as is the case with their love for God the Son. With John's Gospel (but not in his other writings) the word 'agape' is so highly esteemed that human agape for the Father cannot even be remotely envisaged.

The Father loves the disciples, first insofar as they are members of the world that is in need of redemption, and then in a higher sense as 'disciples' who become 'fully mature with the fullness of Christ' (Eph.4:13). The latter, however, is future possibility; but the possibility of the disciples' answers does not even appear on the horizon.

This silence is a powerful witness to the transcendent majesty of the Father. His agape for the world remains unanswered, also his love for the disciples. Even the best possible human answer would be no answer, would not merit being called 'mutual agape.' The source of the Fatherly love lies on an inaccessible mountain peak.

When one has concentrated on this impression of silence, this silence of the evangelist, in regard to human agape for the Father, one is all the more impressed by the magnificent conclusion to Chapter 14:

... because the prince of this world is on his way. He
has not power over me, but the world must be brought
to know that I love the Father and that I am doing
exactly what the Father told me. Come now, let us go
(14:30f).

229

Christ senses the enemies' approach. Is not 'prince of this world' a bold, nearly divinizing, title? It states not only that Satan has managed to find a place in souls but in so doing has gone on to take possession of a part of the world, of creation. Out of the great, unified universe that God penetrates, a certain province seems to have been sundered, in which God's omnipresence and omnipotence have lost their dominance. This realm of existence has become so thoroughly blinded to and walled off from the original divine that intelligent beings can act and think in it as 'atheists.' (Naturally, this disregards the fact that even this 'fallen' province could not exist for a moment if God the Father did not keep it in existence. What we said is not intended absolutely but relatively. God is definitely omnipresent, but there is more or less of this presence, which accounts for the dramatic fluctuation of the human history of rebellion and salvation.)

Christ came not only to save souls but, through them, the world as well (3:17; 4:42; 6:33,51; 12:47). When he once again accepted his death in spite of the horrible consternation in his soul, he knew that this dealt a decisive blow to the prince of this world, that through his sacrifice on the cross the prince of this world had been, in principle, dethroned. 'Now sentence is being passed on this world; now the prince of this world is to be overthrown' (12:31).

As when he underwent his temptation, so too on the eve of Good Friday, Jesus experienced the sinister presence of the Enemy. At the last moment, when he is about to take the final steps of his return 'to the Father,' the Evil One approaches once again. 'The prince of this world is on his way' (14:30). Since his temptation, Christ's spirit has taken increasing possession of his human nature and increasingly sanctified it. There is no longer a point where he is open to attack from him who is evil. 'He has nothing on me.'

That is the unique situation out of which the unique words about Christ's love for the Father are spoken. If we dare say it, Christ needed to feel Satan's breath on his neck before he uttered these words out of the depths of his being. If it had not been for this 'provocation,' they probably would have remained unspoken and never brought to this final stage of consciousness.

One senses remotely how the powers of evil have been given in some way a mission to 'call forth' this highest revelation of divine agape.

With the same breath he speaks of both his love for the Father and his readiness for action, '... and I do' *(poiō)*. This love expresses itself in action, in a deed that will dethrone the 'prince of this world' and reorder the development of the world so that the Father will become 'all in all.' The drive to action vibrates in the 'dynamic' conclusion to the chapter, 'So up, let us go forward!'

25. The agape of the disciples

1. The agape of the disciples for one another

Due to the unusually exalted concept of agape in John's Gospel, it is not until after the thirteenth chapter, when certain presuppositions have been established, that the disciples can even be thought of as loving with agape.

After the Washing of the Feet

John's Gospel contains an intensely dramatic conflict between *light* and *darkness*. Perhaps the most ingenious revelation of the evangelist's artistic use of black and white lies in the dramatic moment of conflict, in the transition from Judas' expulsion to the Farewell Discourses. This is the sequence: the darkness that consumes Judas and the shining forth of a radiant glory in the room of the Last Supper.

> As soon as Judas had taken the piece of bread he went out. Night had fallen. When he had gone Jesus said, 'Now has the Son of Man been glorified, and in him God has been glorified. If God has been glorified in him, God will in turn glorify him in himself, and will glorify him very soon.' (13:30-32).

Through the unusual repetition of the word 'glorify' *(doxazein,* five times in the short text), one acquires the impression that an immeasurable radiance broke out. In the attempt to understand the text more fully, it becomes apparent that this radiance is derived from the rising of not one but three suns.

We have to do with a threefold glorification:
1. The Son of Man is glorified.
2. God is glorified in him (revealed).
3. God will glorify him, the Son of Man, now in himself, in God.

The Son of Man — God in the Son of Man — the Son of Man in God. That is the hierarchy of glorification. The third and final one has yet to happen. It is completed in the Ascension, when man's nature is free from death and devil and given its place in heaven, when not only his soul and spirit but his body as well receives eternal life.

We have already mentioned that before the raising of Lazarus, Christ speaks of the glorification of thy Son of God (11:4), and only when the Greeks approach and Christ feels the proximity of Golgotha does he speak for the first time of the glorification of the Son of Man. 'Now the hour has come for the Son of Man to be glorified' (12:23). This will be continued and powerfully intensified in 13:31.

The being of man, darkened through the first fall, becomes luminous again. In its weakened condition it obscured the divine foundation of the world, but now it begins to become transparent for the light of God.

Man's nature, which was about to succumb to dead matter and the prince of this world, becomes a rightful member of the heavenly world through the Resurrection and Ascension of Christ.

This is the threefold glory of which 13:31 speaks. This illumination, transfiguration, and glorification of man's nature is the presupposition for calling on man, for the first time in John's Gospel after the washing of the feet, to be bearers of agape. This is a counterbalance to Judas' 'mystical union' with Satan and his disappearance into the kingdom of the night (13:30). To the divine potentiality of man is opposed his diabolic one.

I give you a new commandment: *love one another;* just
as I have loved you, *you also must love one another.*

> By this love you have for one another, everyone will
> know that you are my disciples (13:34f, emphasis
> added).

The commandment of love is spoken solemnly in a threefold
form according to its Trinitarian aspects. Its three forms are:

1. a command, or assignment, 'I give you a new commandment ...'
2. dependence on their imitation of Christ's example, 'Just as
   I ...'
3. the promise of an understanding that 'all' will derive from
   it, 'in that way all will know ...'

The first sentence has an authoritarian formulation ('Principle
of the Father'). The second humanizes the commandment for
the disciples by pointing to the example of the Logos become flesh ('Principle of the Son'). The third points to a
knowledge that is intended for all ('Principle of the Spirit').
The assembly of Christianized men, the 'Church,' should be so
luminous that by looking at her this knowledge will be
enkindled for 'all.' We saw this same chain of thought in the
high priestly prayer.

One should not overlook the nuance of the 'giving.' As in
the other passages where John speaks of 'giving,' it has a very
full resonance here, too. We encountered this important
Johannine context of 'giving' the first time in 3:16 ('... that he
gave his only Son'), where it is united with the agape sequence. In order to hear the passage (13:34) properly, it is
necessary to realize that it belongs to the series of passages
that deal with giving, and specifically with Christ's giving.*

* Here are a list of all the things Christ is said to give in John's Gospel,
according to their sequence in the text: Power to become children of God
(1:12), living water (4:10-14), bread (6:11,15; 21:13), fish (6:11; 21:13), food
for eternal life (6:27), his flesh (6:51), eternal life (10:28; 17:2), his example
(13:15), a new commandment (13:34), his peace (14:27), the words *(rhēmata)*
of God (17:8), the word (Logos) of God (17:14), his glory (17:22).

In addition Christ is 'given' a command by his Father in regard to his
speaking and acting. '... what I was to say, what I had to speak, was
commanded by the Father who sent me' (12:49). '... that I am doing exactly
what the Father told me' (14:31).

We have already pointed out that 'commandment' is not to be understood in the Old Testament sense. This will become clearer in the following.

The metaphor of the vine

Following the metaphor of the vine, the commandment of love appears once again in the Eucharistic fifteenth chapter (15:12):

This is my commandment: *love one another,* as I have loved you.

As opposed to the formulation in 13:34, one notices that here John wrote 'my' instead of 'new' commandment. 'My commandment.' 'New' — 'My.'

'New' (*kainos,* not *neos*) does not mean anything superficial like 'an eleventh commandment in addition to the other ten,' but has a more qualitative significance. As in many other passages in the New Testament it wants to point to something 'specifically Christian.' One might say that the newness was not 'formal' but 'material' — newness in content. With Christ's 'I am,' the epitome of all sources and origins appears on earth. When this 'I' expresses its life, one sees that it emerges immediately from the sphere of the divine Creator. Everything that comes in contact with this 'I' receives the character of divine originality; it is 'renewed.' This is expressed by such phrases as 'new creature,' 'new heaven and earth,' and 'behold, I make all things new.'

We would misunderstand Christ if, when he spoke of the 'new commandment,' we were to search anxiously through the history of religion to see if perhaps someone else had given the commandment of love before him. As many others as may have given it, it is 'new' because Christ gives it and in his 'I' he bears the power to transform and renew the world. Its 'newness' lies in the saying, 'just as I have loved you,' and 'in that way all men will know that you are my disciples,' disciples of my ego (emphasized in the Greek: *emoi mathētai).* Earlier we explained that this emphatic 'my' in John's Gospel is to be understood in the light of the Johannine 'I am' statements.

Thus it is not surprising that in the repetition of the commandment of love in the fifteenth chapter, 'new' can be replaced by the emphatic 'my': 'This is my commandment' — the sentence sets a goal for the disciples that emerges from the 'I am' of Christ.

It is precisely the fifteenth chapter, almost more than any other, that is filled with 'mysteries of the ego.' It is introduced by the seventh and final Johannine 'I am' statement: 'I am the true vine.'* After it follow all the passages about 'I' and 'my' in which the vine of Christ glows and the mystery of the chalice of his blood radiates. 'Every branch in me' (15:2), 'make your home in me' (15:3), 'I am the vine' (15:4), 'cut off from me you can do nothing' (15:5), 'if anyone who does not remain in me' (15:6), 'if you remain in me' (15:7), 'and you will be my disciples' (15:8), 'so I have loved you' (15:9), 'remain in my love' (15:9), 'Just as I have kept my Father's commandments' (15:10), 'so that my own joy may be you' (15:11).

'My commandment' in 15:12 must be seen in this context.

Before the transition is made from the theme of mystical unity to that of the hatred the disciples will undergo, Jesus summarizes his proclamation about love in the brief pregnant sentence:

What I command you is to love one another (15:17).
Here the noun 'commandment' is replaced by the verb 'command.' It becomes thereby a more personal, immediate address to the disciples.

All of these passages have in common the reference to the setting of a goal, to a 'command.' This agape 'for one another' does not yet exist. It is still pre-existent in the Spirit of Christ.

---

* Bread (6:35), light (8:12), door (10:7), shepherd (10:11), resurrection and the life (11:25), the way, the truth, and the life (14:6), the vine (15:1). Rittelmeyer was the first to point out this sevenfold organism.

2. The agape of the disciples for Christ

The Promises

Love of Christ is not a 'commission' like brotherly love. According to the strict, unillusioned, sober understanding of John's Gospel the latter can be only a later fruit of Christian development. But the agape for Christ, which has been placed before the eyes of Christians in all its divine and human glory, is expected to be the basic disposition of the disciples.

Thus it is simply stated in the fourteenth chapter, 'If you love me.'

If you love me you will keep my commandments
(14:15, emphasis added).

True Christian activity originates in love for Christ. The 'keeping of the commandments,' the 'goals,' includes the activity of consistent, faithful meditation as well as the proper exterior deeds. All other motives for activity, such as the fear of hell, are beneath the Christian standard. Love for Christ is the driving force behind the development of a Christian personality. It leads into the kingdom of the Holy Spirit by creating the proper presuppositions for the proper knowledge of the truth. The quoted sentence continues: 'I shall ask the Father, and he will give you another Advocate *[paraklēton]* to be with you forever ... that Spirit of truth ...'

The following passages no longer say 'you.' The promise in 14:15 is general and applies to all Christians. Now we see more clearly how the treading of this path is the concern of each individual. Thus the plural is replaced by the singular. The transition is not from plural to singular 'you' but to the distant 'third person.' There are numerous sentences in John's Gospel that begin this way, 'of anyone ...' or 'Whoever (does this or that) ...' (A participial construction in Greek: 'the one doing this or that ...') For example: 'I am the living bread which has come down from heaven. Anyone who eats this bread will live for ever' (6:51). Or: 'I am the light of the world; anyone who follows me [the one following after me] will not be walking in the dark' (8:12). This form of speech has a specific person in mind, a certain 'somebody.' The hearer is not immediately exhorted to do this or that; it is left entirely up to him whether or not he wants to be this 'somebody,' this 'whoever.' Christ communicates merely a higher lawfulness, a propriety of the higher world. The hearer must decide on his own whether or not to apply it to his own person. Even this tender reverence for human freedom is related to the 'I' character of John's Gospel.

Anyone who receives my commandments and keeps

them, *will be one who loves me.'* (14:21)

With all possible emphasis Christian activity is presented as the hallmark of those who truly love Christ. It is given the emphatic position at the end of the sentence; 'he [in the original the strongly emphatic *ekeinos,* 'that one'] it is, who loves me.'

The sentence in 14:15 allows the deed to proceed from the love; 14:21 leads again from the deed to the love. Perhaps not only in the sense that the confirmation of love through action is once again strongly emphasized, but also that Christian activity continually deepens one's love for Christ. The way in which heaven opens up in response to such striving is described in the very next sentence.

Anybody who loves me will be loved by my Father ...

and I shall love him and show myself to him (14:21).

This flowing of the agape of the Father and the Son is finally intensified to a full experience of *Communion.*

Judas, not the Iscariot, had asked why the revelation of Christ was not to take place before all the world. He failed to see that Jesus could reveal his glory only to loving eyes. Just as in ordinary life a man cannot reveal himself unless another shows openness and receptivity, so too, and even more so, in the world beyond the senses. There is no disinterested looking that simply sees everything that is visible. Vision is given only to the eyes of the lover. In the realm of the spiritual, love does not make one blind but opens his eyes.

Judas still lacked this intimate knowledge. In response to his question Christ concludes the chain of thought begun in 14:21:

> If anyone loves me he will keep my word, and my
> Father will love him, and we shall come to him and
> make our home with him.*

In response to Judas' concern about world opinion, Jesus emphasizes that he is first of all concerned with the individual and his interior experience. The redemption of the world must begin in the interior of the individual. 'If anyone ...' This time the keeping of the 'commandments' is replaced by the keeping of 'my word' (Logos). This transfers even more the notion of Christian activity into the realm of the interior and the spiritual. This strong emphasis on the 'meditation on the word' returns even more directly to the root of proper outward conduct. Now Father and Son are combined in a divine 'We.' It is the plural of the divine fullness and at the same time the plural of the community of love within God. Heaven's mystery of love reveals itself on the level of communion ('make our home with him'). The mystical union of man with God permits simultaneously the experience of the inner-Trinitarian 'We,' which includes the mystical union of the Father with the Son. 'We will come to him' and 'make our home with him.' This is a reversal of the sentence at the beginning of the fourteenth chapter, 'There are many rooms in my Father's house' (14:2). The one verse speaks of the multitude of men being given roots and protection in the one divine ground. The other speaks of the fullness of the divine dwelling in the individual man. The Greek middle form also says this: 'for our sake' we will make of him 'our' dwelling *(poiēsometha).*

---

* As translated from Frieling.

The lack of agape

These passages, 14:15, 21, and 23, have shown how agape for Christ consecrates the disciples even to the point of communion, where man becomes the dwelling of the divine fullness. The Greek word for 'dwelling' is *monē*, which is the noun derived from the verb meaning 'to remain'; we have already shown this important Johannine concept. Thus it means here 'a lasting abode' or 'a lasting place to remain.'

But the sketch of this line of development has passed beyond the reality of the moment. The disciples cannot yet be said to have agape for Christ. This is shown not so much by 14:24 ('Those who do not love me do not keep my words'), for this verse expresses merely a general possibility without specifically applying it to the disciples.* But it can be seen clearly in 14:28:

> *If you loved me* you would have been glad to know that
> I am going to the Father ...

These words sound resigned. This is the contrary-to-fact usage: 'Those who loved me,' that is, 'but as a matter of fact you do not.' Christ acknowledges the disciples 'philein' for him (16:27) 'because the Father himself loves you for loving me.' This love is not to be scorned, since it is said of God the

---

* It shows 'negatively' the meaning of agape for Christian activity. It is the driving force along the way of consecration that leads to the rebirth of man.

The relation of agape and rebirth confronts us from another perspective in 8:42. Jesus challenges the Jews in Jerusalem, 'If God were your father, you would love me.' This is a 'negative' indication of the importance of rebirth for the life of agape. (It is only through the rebirth as described in 1:12 and 3:3,5,7 that the Jews, who believe their relation to the world of heaven to be guaranteed by their descent from Abraham, will in truth receive God as their Father.)

Does this not leave us with a circle? First rebirth through love and then love through rebirth. We are, however, dealing with two vital processes that occur simultaneously and foster one another; they cannot be definitely classified in the categories of cause and effect. According to the perspective, either the origin of love in rebirth or of rebirth in love is emphasized. It is easy to see why rebirth is emphasized to the Jews, who boast of their descent from Abraham; and agape, to the disciples.

Father himself. The comparison with 16:27 gives us an idea of how exalted the concept of agape is in John's Gospel.

The disciples' agape for Christ should have shown itself in their 'joy' over his return to the Father. As divine love, agape is concerned above all with the salvation of the beloved and the suffering that is involved in attaining this high goal; and as long as he is moving toward it, he lives in the most interior joy despite all pain. We encountered something similar in the story of the raising of Lazarus.

Chapter 14:28 shows more shockingly than any other the heroic and austere side of the agape.

The resigned 'if' — 'if you loved me' — is a transition to the two final passages in our series, which likewise point to the absence of agape.

In the conversation by the lake the risen Christ asks Peter if he loves him.

This is the only time that agape is spoken of in the form of a question. Let us look at the context. It is preceded by the miraculous catch of fish during which John spoke the words of recognition: 'It is the Lord.' After the catch comes a meal. The mood pervading this meal on the shore of the lake in the early morning glow is one of mystery. The disciples see a charcoal fire burning, as well as bread and fish — bread and fish as at the feeding of the five thousand. Likewise this early meal has the character of a Eucharistic mystery. About the feeding of the five thousand, John writes: 'Then Jesus took the loaves, gave thanks *[eucharistēsas],* and gave them out to all who were sitting ready; he then did the same with the fish ...' (6:11).

About the early morning meal, he writes: 'Jesus then stepped forward, took the bread and gave it to them, and the same with the fish' (21:13).

Both descriptions are obviously stylized according to the words used to describe the institution of the Eucharist. There are a few minor differences: nothing is said about 'blessing' at the early morning meal, and it begins with the 'coming' of Jesus: 'Jesus came and took ...'

The feeding of the five thousand took place before the death and resurrection of Christ, and thus before what John calls the 'glorification' of the Son of Man. It is a prophetic event.

The early morning meal takes place after the 'glorification.' It clearly transpires in the sphere of the resurrection, of the realm beyond the senses. This renders superfluous the special Eucharistic blessing that, in consecrating the earthly, elevates it beyond the senses. The world of the miraculous and of the heavenly blessing is simply presupposed to be open. The important point is that the realm beyond the senses draws sufficiently close to man on earth and is experienced vividly enough as a reality. Therefore, the taking and giving of the bread is introduced by the coming of Jesus. The risen Christ had already called to the disciples, 'Come and have breakfast.' If we considered only the external situation, it would be hard to understand this emphasis on 'coming.' This is changed as soon as we realize that John is describing here delicate events that surpass the senses. There are degrees to which we experience a being we cannot sense. The impression from this meeting can be stronger or weaker, more or less conscious. The being that reveals itself can appear either 'farther' or 'nearer,' whereby 'far' and 'near' do not refer to quantitative space but to the greater or less reality the being seems to have. The disciples should come: they should 'move themselves' with their own activity toward the event. The risen Christ 'is coming'; the disciples consciousness of his nearness is intensified. This awareness of his greater nearness is then combined with the actual Eucharistic event: 'He came up, took the bread, and gave it to them.'

A similar intensification of an experience that surpasses the senses and is expressed in terms of a spatial drawing-near occurs in Matthew 28:18. The risen Christ appears but some of the disciples 'doubt.' Their 'seeing' is so weak that it cannot give them the certainty that they are confronting a reality. 'Jesus came up and spoke to them.' The encounter becomes more intense and has within itself the evidence of a real experience. One can also detect an uncertainty among the disciples in our text (John 21). Looking at the sentence logically, purely from the viewpoint of formal logic, we have to admit that it contains a contradiction, but psychologically it expresses perfectly a simultaneous knowing and yet not-knowing: 'None of the disciples was bold enough to ask "Who are you?" They knew quite well it was the Lord.' This recognition that the beloved disciple first expressed, 'It is the Lord' (21:7) is adopted unquestioningly by the others because of the sacred meal. Jesus' coming to the meal is a more and more clearly resounding 'I am,' and for the disciples a clearer and clearer 'He is.'

All of this provides the necessary preparation for the question addressed to Peter.

After the meal Jesus said to Simon Peter, 'Simon son of John, *do you love [agapas] me more than these others do?'* (21:15, emphasis added).

The first word that breaks the 'ban of silence' — the event of the meal took place in the silence of a mystery; the first word spoken out of the presence of the risen Christ, as it becomes more and more real, is this question about agape.

It is well known how intimately the early Christians associated 'meal' and 'agape.' In giving them to eat, Christ reveals most fully the mystery of his agape, of the surrender of his being — the mystery that is therefore repeatedly proclaimed in the sacrament of the altar.

The experience of Christ's substantial, nurturing agape in his 'third' appearance before the disciples (21:14) prepares Peter to hear and be struck by this threefold accusing question.

The question is definitely accusing; it has often been recognized that this threefold question had to call to mind Peter's threefold denial.

On the eve of Good Friday, Peter had spoken generously, 'I will lay down my life for you' (13:37). These words, which we saw to be intimately related to agape (10:17; 15:13), Christ repeats, 'Will you indeed lay down your life for me?'

as if he wanted to make Peter fully aware of what he had said. He then predicts the threefold denial after the crowing of the cock.

If Peter at that time had had the right to say what he did, he would have been able to answer the question of the risen Christ: 'Yes, I love you with agape.' As it is he must forgo the use of this exalted word and restrict himself to *philia:* 'Yes Lord, you know that I have affection *[philō]* for you.' He felt he had the right to say that (compare 16:27: 'because you have affection for me'). In his answers he does not mention the 'more than all these others do' and thus it is dropped in the second question:

Simon son of John, *Do you love [agapas] me?* (21:16, emphasis added).

Christ asks him once again for agape. Peter answers again: 'Yes, Lord, you know that I have affection *[philō]* for you.' Once again he forgoes using the exalted word and assures Christ of his *philia.*

Thus it is all the more painful when Christ himself, in the third question, descends to the level of *philia* with the words: 'Simon son of John, do you love *[phileis]* me?' and thereby places even that kind of love in question.

Summary

The fundamental threefold division that we noticed in the first survey — agape of the Father, agape of Christ, agape of the disciples — was further subdivided when we asked about the object, the 'whom' of agape in addition to the subject, the 'who.' This resulted in various relations of agape:

1. The agape of the *Father* which applies to the world (3:16). The agape of the Father which applies to the Son (3:35; 10:17; 15:9f; 17:23,24,26). The agape of the Father which applies to the disciples (14:21-23; 17:23-26).

2. The agape of the *Son* which applies to the disciples (11:5;

13:1,23; 19:26; 21:7,20 and 13:34; 14:21; 15:9,10,12,13). The agape of the Son which applies to the Father (14:31).

3. The agape of the *disciples:* which should apply to one another (13:34,35; 15:12,17); which should apply to Christ (14:15,21,23,28; 21:15f).

Thus we see that there are seven such relationships of agape in John's Gospel. (Apparently even the individual passages are ordered according to sacred numbers. The seven reappears frequently [the love of the Father for the Son; of the Son for the disciples, in two sevenfold series; of the disciples for Christ]; in divisions 1 and 3 it is increased by five to make twelve.)

In all of these what remains unsaid is, as we have seen, just as important as what is said. What agape is in John's Gospel becomes clear only when the various passages have been assembled. Only that agape is the subject of our study. Agape is something different in the other books of the New Testament, even in John's first Epistle, which is closest in content and language to John's Gospel. Agape appears there both as a noun and as a verb more often than in all twenty-one chapters of the Gospel. But in the Epistle, agape is not conceived of so strictly and exclusively, which can be seen for instance in the unquestioned presupposition of the disciples' agape for God.

The five negative passages — 3:19; 5:42; 8:42; 12:43; 12:25 — were not mentioned in the survey but have been discussed in the appropriate contexts. It is a very special concept which, with this meaning, is proper only to the Fourth Gospel. It is a complex thought that one cannot easily master at the first try. Rather, one is dealing with a living organism. This study has pointed out the various functions, in detail, but it cannot be concluded without reminding the reader that these various functions are the expressions of the life of a unified whole.

Bibliography

Bock, Emil, *The Three Years,* Floris, Edinburgh 1980.

Bornkamm, Günther, *Jesus of Nazareth,* 1956. First English edition Hodder & Stoughton, London 1960.

Bultmann, Rudolf, *Theologie des Neuen Testamentes.*

Frieling. Rudolf, *Christianity and Reincarnation,* Floris, Edinburgh 1977.

Frieling, Rudolf, *Old Testament Studies,* Floris, Edinburgh 1987.

Lohmeyer, E., *Das Evangelium des Markus.*

Wistinghausen, Kurt von, *Das neue Bekenninis — Wege zum Credo.* Urachhaus, Stuttgart 1983.

Index to biblical references

INDEX TO BIBLICAL REFERENCES

Index

INDEX

INDEX